DAYS
LIKE
THESE

'Pip's words are like a knowing hug of reassurance telling you everything is going to be OK, and making you think kind thoughts about yourself and the parenting you're doing.'
CHRISSIE SWAN

This book is dedicated to every mum who has lain awake, worrying about a child.

Pip Lincolne

DAYS LIKE THESE

A comforting, practical companion for tired and terrific mums

murdoch books
Sydney | London

Contents

Introduction 6

•

1. LOOKING OUT FOR YOURSELF 8
When you feel like you're
on your own

2. YOU CAN DO THIS 42
When you're feeling
overwhelmed

3. CHANGING YOUR EXPECTATIONS 64
When you're drowning
in mum guilt

4. THE LONG GAME 84
When you need a reminder
of the magic you're making

5. MUMS MATTER 106
When you've forgotten
who YOU are

6. JOIN THE CLUB 130
When you feel like you've
really messed up

7. YOU'RE A GREAT MUM 152
When your best doesn't
feel like it's enough

8. BEYOND TIRED 168
When you feel like you're
doing all the work

9. YOU AND ME BOTH 190
When other people are
getting you down

10. YOU ARE NOT ALONE 210
When you need some
expert help

11. DIAMOND DAYS AHEAD 230
When you're wondering if
there's more to life

•

Playlist for mums 254
Reading list 256
Support services 258
Thanks to ... 259
Index 260

Introduction

Mums face unique challenges and demands as they navigate the twenty or more years it can take to raise and release a human out into the world. But for some reason, they often get forgotten in the juggle to bring up babies, children, teenagers and young adults. This nonsense must stop! Honestly, how is it that there is not a slew of books encouraging mums to love and look after themselves?

The good news is that if we look after mums – and help them to care for themselves – then everyone in the family reaps the benefits.

Days Like These is the perfect book-shaped care package to tuck into the hands of your favourite mum. (That could be YOU! Or maybe it's a lovely friend or family member?) It's for those sometimes forgotten mums who spend a giant chunk of their lives looking after others. I'm talking about the kind who love the people they brought into the world, but also find themselves thinking stuff like, 'Am I doing this right?' and 'When will I ever get a moment to myself?' and 'Oh my gosh I stuffed up everything today!' or 'Who am I, now that my pre-mum life is a distant memory?' or possibly, 'How did I manage to raise such a tall (and at times sarcastic) young person?'

I'm in a pretty great spot to be pushing these important looking-after-mum lessons. I have raised three kids of my own, both with a partner and without at various times. My kiddos are all grown up now – in their twenties and thirties – and are lovely humans, making their own way in the world, so it seemed like a brilliant time to reflect, share and talk through the triumphs and tricky bits of mum life.

Whether you're co-parenting, parenting with a partner or parenting solo, this book has bright ideas on how to make sense of the scramble and find meaning in the mess, no matter which stage of parenting you are deep within. Be that the 'yes, you really do have to wear pants to child care' years or the 'what do you mean there's another excursion?' years or the 'get off that screen' years or even the 'I'd love to talk more about TikTok' years.

I have spent the past twenty years parenting my own kids through all of these phases, as well as writing for major parenting media outlets about the ins and outs of various fads and pressures. So make yourself a cup of tea. Grab three biscuits. Let's talk about big and brilliant mum/woman stuff.

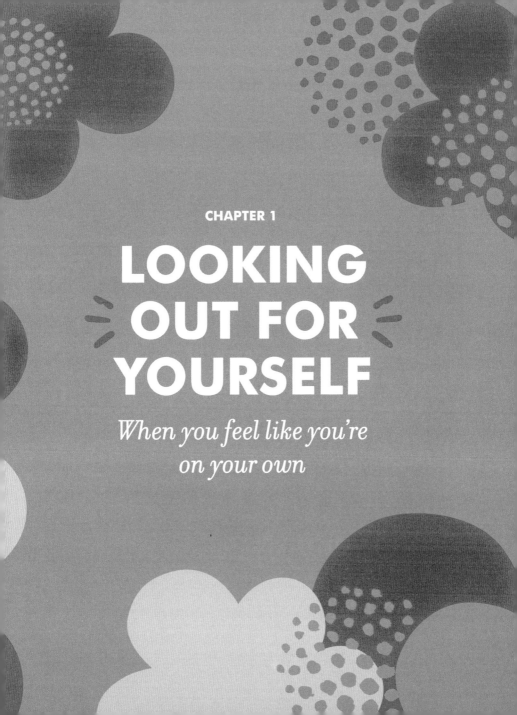

CHAPTER 1

LOOKING OUT FOR YOURSELF

When you feel like you're on your own

Putting 'mum life' into perspective

Mum life is the marathon you didn't realise you'd signed up to run. What started as a maternal urge or a happy accident becomes reality around nine months later and then it doesn't let up … ever!

I have not typed those words to upset you, but rather to give you a nifty framework that really will provide some often much-needed perspective during those lifelong days.

This mum marathon is – like all actual marathons – a challenge to your physical and mental health. Your head and heart and other human bits take turns to hurt at designated times. Sometimes they hurt all together, which can be especially distressing.

THE GOOD NEWS IS THAT:

a) You are not alone and there are millions of others who are quietly running the marathon alongside you.

b) There are lots of ways you can support your health (both physical and emotional) as you move through your days.

The other good news (yes, there is even more!) is that you are going to learn so much about yourself and the world on this marathon, if only you can manage to come to terms with the fact that you are possibly running even more slowly than you would walk.

You don't need me to tell you that the best way to complete a marathon is to be in top shape. Stretchy pants will assist you no end on your mum marathon, but so will self-supporting as well as enlisting the help of others.

A self-supporting strategy

What is self-supporting, I hear you ask? It's a strategy for noticing what's going on with your good self and making your own health and happiness an absolute priority as you navigate parenthood.

This admittedly goes against a lot of what we've been told about being a mother. In fact, the very idea might make you shudder a little. ('Won't somebody think of the children?' Of course we will. We love them. But this book is about us, not them.)

We've been told that being a mum is all about sacrifice and we've been encouraged to quietly suck up any pain or struggles we may have and simply push on.

This strategy results in, at the very best, run-down and tired mums and, at worst, mums with an interconnected range of physical and mental health concerns. It's fair to say that there is nothing helpful about those attitudes of old, and it's time for us to do a giant reset. While children are very, very important, they are certainly not more important than a mother's wellbeing.

If you are a mum reading this right now – and chances are that you are – it's absolutely vital for you to know that you and your health and happiness are not something to be pushed aside or ignored. Your days are supposed to have good things dotted through them and you are meant to feel as well as possible. It's not *all* about your kids.

When my first child was a preschooler I found myself getting more and more unwell, both physically and mentally. I was just a kid myself in many ways, at the time. Only twenty years old and clearly struggling with parenthood, but determined to make it work. As I became more physically unwell with a multitude of colds, viruses, asthma flare-ups and more, I tried to reach out to those around me about my mental health concerns.

'The doctor said I need more rest,' I said to some family and friends. What this actually meant was, 'I am feeling incredibly overwhelmed and unwell and my mental health is suffering and I would like to sleep for 127 years', but this was when discussion around mental health was not as open as it is now. The response was, 'You need to look after yourself' and similar, and that was maddening because dammit I wanted someone to look after *me* for a change.

This situation became upsettingly familiar as my firstborn grew older, and it happened when my second and third were little and school aged, too. It became clear to me that while the people around me loved me, when push came to shove nobody was going to look after me and this was very bloody distressing. Clearly many mums have wonderful partners who want to contribute as best they can. But sometimes the people around you can't quite fathom the relentlessness of parenting and just how much you need their help. They figure you can just fix yourself up with things like daily exercise, several full nights' sleep and green veggies for dinner every night. Sorted!

Of course, this is not the bloody case, although those things (when they are possible) can help a bit. The fact is, there are one thousand (possibly more) different complications and circumstances to navigate when you are a parent. It's not as simple as getting a good night's sleep, as brilliant as that would be. Support – and self-supporting – are key.

10 SIMPLE WAYS TO SELF-SUPPORT

1. Spend a little bit of time writing down where you are at each day – not a to-do list, but more of a check-in with how you're doing overall, what is and isn't working, and the progress you are making.

2. Check in with yourself. Ask yourself how you are feeling each day. Think about how to look after yourself accordingly, even if it's just doing little things to make the day easier.

3. Check in with your body. Try using a guided meditation app such as Insight Timer and take five minutes to relax before you go to sleep (or at another quieter time of the day).

4. Do less. Shed as many responsibilities as you can and rethink all the activities you (and your children) spend time doing.

5. Make soup! Make a giant batch of vegetable soup a couple of times a week – this way you'll always have something healthy and nourishing on stand-by.

6. Forgive yourself. If you bugger something up, remember that you are human and that humans make mistakes (more about mistakes in Chapter 6).

7. Schedule downtime. It can be really hard to prioritise time to yourself or time away from your family, but – as I am sure you know – it's an excellent way to bolster wellbeing.

8. See your doctor regularly. If you have a therapist, same goes for them. It's really important to maintain your wellbeing and very easy to forget to do this, or to prioritise your child's health instead of your own. Let's not do that!

9. Know that you need strong relationships with a couple of other humans to feel your very best. Even the most introverted or self-reliant person needs others in their life. Look after the friendships and family connections that matter most to you.

10. Write down three good things that happened each day. It's a proven mood-booster.

A little help from my friends

Children are the responsibility of their parents, but also the responsibility of their broader family and the community. It takes a village, as they say. If we don't look after each other – not only children and caregivers, but also the elderly and the vulnerable – then we are not looking after society as a whole.

That's all well and good and very important to note, but if you are a mum, many of the people around you are probably too busy with their own lives to check in with how you are going.

'Where is my village?', you might be wondering, and you'd be right to do so. This lack of support is a sad reality for many, many mums. Some of us *do* have family and friends who are keen to step up and may not even need to be asked. But generally mums are not getting the help they need and find it really hard to ask for support. For some, their support structure is not nearby and they may make do with keeping in touch remotely. For others, family relationships are complicated and asking for help seems pretty much impossible. Perhaps YOU are one of those mums?

I have been one of those mums, struggling under the weight of parental challenges, but feeling like asking for help might alert those around me to my flaws and prompt intimacy with people that I don't feel quite ready for.

If you are wishing you had more help but are either unable to access it (due to circumstance or complex relationships) or feel too embarrassed to ask for it, please know that finding a way to build support into your life is vital! Not only will feeling supported make your days peachier, you'll be modelling excellent behaviour to your kids and also providing them with an extended support network. Sounds like a brilliant plan, doesn't it?

The loneliness link

Everyone is different. For some of us, asking for help is easy. Perhaps this is related to the support structure that is already around us.

For most of us, however, asking for help is just the hardest thing. For starters we might feel that we don't have anyone to ask, and there are other complicating factors, too. We worry that people will think we're not coping, worry about being judged, worry about someone calling the authorities on us because we are clearly the worst parent EVER. And mostly ... we feel terribly alone in our struggle. As writer and broadcaster Jamila Rizvi says in her book, *The Motherhood*, 'The loneliness of modern mothers isn't the exception – it's the rule.'

It's not just in the newborn phase and early years that this isolation hits hard. As children grow older, those visitors who loved popping in and holding your cute, fresh baby drop off and very often you find yourself alone in the wilderness of parenting a non-baby or deep in the unbridled confusion of parenting a fully fledged teenager.

People seem to assume that because your child is alive and growing, you have totally got it all together. Chances are, if you are reading this book, that simply isn't the case (and even if you are not reading this book, for that matter). Where you may have sobbed into your tiny baby's hair and wondered if they will ever, ever sleep (answer: yes, one day!), you now have a schoolkid or a teenager and not only will they not let you sob on their scalp, they are quite likely to throw a sneaker at you and slam the door in your face, if you ever try to do so.

Anthropologists call the transition to motherhood *matrescence* (more on that in Chapter 3). Most of the discourse we read and hear about this shift is related to newborns and toddlers. That's great, because we love newborns and toddlers. However, the parents of non-babies also find themselves with all kinds of challenges as their kids grow older. Yet the older they grow, the more the helpful chatter, support and information dries up. It's a terrible, crying shame.

This is why forums on websites like Reddit and Mumsnet are packed full of distressed posts with titles like, 'I want to run away' and 'I hate being a mum' and 'I am just so lonely' and 'I have made a huge mistake' and 'My child hates me'. They're written in desperation, often in the dead of night or during a rushed lunch hour, from the heart – both hopeful and hopeless at the same time. They're written by mothers who love their children but are also deep in some of parenting's darkest moments. They're usually feeling alone, ashamed, inadequate, judged and a bit – or a lot – broken. They cannot imagine how they can sort out the issue at hand and doubt they'll emerge unscathed.

And look, it's likely they won't, but that is not necessarily a bad thing. There is something to be learned in every struggle, even if it's just the knowledge that somehow you managed to get through it and are a resilient champion. The hard stuff can help us understand ourselves better and grow stronger, for ourselves and for our kids. I know this sounds like a cliché, but clichés are very often grounded in truth and this is one of those times.

You are not alone in these hard and lonely moments trying to look after your child and yourself. Not by a very long shot.

A 2018 Relationships Australia report, 'Is Australia experiencing an epidemic of loneliness?', found that one in ten Australians lack social support and one in six live with emotional loneliness. These people don't have the meaningful relationships in their lives that would help sustain and nurture them. Add a kid (or two or more) to this isolated mix and these many, many lonely people have an awful lot to contend with.

Feeling unsupported as well as being unable to ask for help is a sort of gateway for lots of different and negative health implications. I tell you this because I want you to know how important it is to work out this isolating situation and find ways to form meaningful relationships and get what you need from the people around you.

Research tells us that loneliness and exhaustion intertwine with physical and mental ill health and, before you know it, they're crafting an environment of crappiness. Each of these tricky issues unhelpfully gives momentum to the other until you feel tied up in knots and unsure of where to start untangling what's really going on. It all feels like a whopping mess. (The good news is that we can unravel it. So don't lose hope – keep reading!)

Being isolated and lonely – something that many, many mums experience – has a huge impact on women. We're learning more and more about this every day, with research telling us that loneliness is as bad for us as smoking and a bunch of other undesirable health conditions. For starters, loneliness can prompt that helpful-yet-pesky 'fight or flight' stress response, negatively affecting the immune system and potentially causing inflammation-related health conditions and other physical and mental health issues. Before you know it, stress hormones such as cortisol and norepinephrine are firing. Not content with powering fear and anxiety, they're also keen to pop in when we're feeling lonely. As you can imagine, all this hormonal and emotional toing and froing can take a toll.

In a 2018 *Irish Times* article, 'Mental health and isolation: The lonely road of parenthood', psychologist Aisling Leonard-Curtin discussed the potential consequences. 'When loneliness and isolation happen on an on-going basis for parents, they are far more susceptible to anxiety, depression and burnout,' she explained. 'It can also have an impact on our physical well-being, decreasing our immunity to common colds and flus whilst also increasing our chances of experiencing back, neck and headaches.'

Dr Nicole Valtorta, a Newcastle University epidemiologist, led a 2016 study linking loneliness with a 30 per cent increase in the risk of stroke or development of coronary heart disease. 'Lacking encouragement from family or friends, those who are lonely may slide into unhealthy habits,' Dr Valtorta said in an American Psychological Association article, 'The risks of social isolation'. 'In addition', she said, 'loneliness has been found to raise levels of stress, impede sleep and, in turn, harm the body. Loneliness can also augment depression or anxiety.'

As you can see, the very act of becoming a parent – and the feelings of isolation and worry this inevitably brings – predisposes you to some negative health consequences. This is why it's so very important to put yourself first, find ways to feel better supported and strengthen your connections to other humans.

Have a good natter

The phrase 'find your tribe' is pretty ubiquitous, right up there with 'join the conversation' in terms of marketing speak. But the fact remains that friendship and support from other humans are invaluable when you're a mum.

When we have kids, the existing friendships we have often change and the research tells us that seeking out new friends who also have kids can make a big difference to how we feel about parenting and life in general.

Lancaster University's Professor Anne Cronin has done some in-depth research into friendships between mothers and confirms that these connections play a valuable and vital part in women's lives. She found that mum friendships boost women's sense of worth and belonging. Not only that, they are extra special because they encourage inclusiveness, intimacy and caring for each other. Perhaps you have discovered this for yourself.

When my kids were small, I didn't have a lot of friends who had kids. I felt a bit isolated by my relationship at the time. It was a challenging union and there didn't seem to be much time or headspace for anyone else. It's the way challenging relationships go, much of the time.

I was also a bit shy to reach out to others, due to my own insecurities, I think. Had I reached out, I would have had a much more well-rounded experience of parenting, one that might have helped me to feel better supported and happier. Coulda, shoulda, woulda, as they say.

Luckily, I can flag this with you as a bit of a fail on my part, and stress to you how important your own friendships are when you are raising kids. It's not all about your kids' pals. Mum pals are equally vital and very much worth prioritising.

There are lots of ways to make friends with other parents or like-minded souls. There are opportunities via the school gate or childcare drop-off zone. There are apps that will connect you to mums who are 'just like you'. There are mums in the park or the library or the office. Mums are all around us!

Clearly what you want, however, is to actually find a mum or two that you have a lot in common with. You're looking for the sort of mums who you'd be friends with even if you didn't have kids.

The benefits of having mum pals cannot be underestimated. You can talk about all the things your child and/or partner is doing to annoy the crap out of you. You can gain a broader understanding of how children develop. And you can get a firsthand squiz at how other people parent.

All of this provides helpful perspective, reassuring you that you are not the only mother in the world who gets sick to death of playing Lego or watching kid movies. You're not the only one who would prefer not to go to the playground, can't do maths homework, finds it hard to listen to extended child monologues or might struggle to be enthusiastic about a teenager's lastest gaming level-up.

Of course, it's not always easy to make friends, and sometimes other issues such as living somewhere quite isolated or living with anxiety or depression make it even harder. This is where online friendships may fill the gap. These might be forged via forums or social media and they may even result in important lifelong connections.

Back in 2015, social scientist Kate Davis studied Australian Facebook mothers' groups for her thesis. She noted how important these – and other social media or online mothers' groups – are to many women.

'Mothers place high value on information shared by others who have had similar experiences,' Kate explained in her thesis. 'They value people with whom they have experiential overlap as information sources. While some participants spoke about valuing advice from health professionals, it was clear that the recounted experiences of other mothers were extremely important sources of information and that the mothers trusted these shared experiences.'

Kate noted that being part of this interconnected sisterhood was one of the unexpected benefits that many of the mums she spoke to loved about parenting. These women spoke of a sense of solidarity, of qualifying for a community and feeling connected to other mums – 'belonging to an amorphous community of mothers that transcends geography, time zones, platforms and spaces; participating in both online and offline mothers' groups.'

This community has all kinds of proven benefits for mums and their kiddos. A recent study of over a thousand mother–child pairs found that children of women with larger social networks benefited developmentally.

Study co-author Kaja LeWinn is a psychiatry researcher at the University of California, San Francisco, and she noted that mums with larger social networks reap all sorts of rewards thanks to this supportive people power. What Kaja and her colleagues call a 'community-based social life' seems to reduce parenting stress and boost mental wellbeing in mums.

HOW TO MAKE FRIENDS WITH OTHER MUMS

1. Be yourself … because look how great you are!

2. Spend time at school (you could volunteer if you have time) where you're likely to meet other mums.

3. Join local kid/parent-focused groups – sporty, creative, fitness-focused or other.

4. Introduce yourself to other mums when you encounter them. Assume that they are looking for pals, too! Be bold, if you can.

5. Search Facebook for interest groups in your area. You are likely to encounter other parents there … and possibly find opportunities for new friendships.

6. Be friendly when you are down at the local shops or park or library. Perhaps your new best friend is lurking there.

7. Keep trying! Don't give up if your first efforts are awkward. Your perfect mum-friend match is waiting out there for you, somewhere.

Dear Pip

'Things aren't going so well right now.'

At some point you might become aware that you're not feeling so good. And now that you think of it, maybe you've been feeling like that for a little or a long while. When my own mental health was in crisis, I saw the first signs in my physical body. I avoided going to the doctor and instead tried to manage lowered immunity, headaches, sore back, sore neck, weight gain, bad skin and a plethora of other illnesses, a new condition rolling in before I'd had a chance to recover from the previous one.

This is very typical when you are a mum. You're under pressure and society has taught you that if you get your child's issues and concerns sorted, then your own wellbeing will fall into place next. Perhaps you are already nodding wildly as you read?

What society should be doing is flipping that thinking and realising that healthy mums are in a much better position to have healthy kids than blinking exhausted mums. And we should all be thinking about ways we can support mums in their quest for feeling okay enough to face each day.

Research has found that pain, fatigue and emotional wellbeing are intertwined and that when we are feeling physically well, we are more likely to feel emotionally well. The reverse is also true – when we are emotionally peaky, our bodies feel peaky, too.

Science is still trying to work out exactly how the whole mind and body wellbeing two-step really works. They think that some physical health changes in our bodies could be impacted by a bunch of different factors such as:

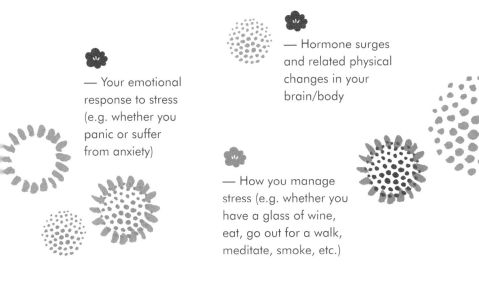

— Your emotional response to stress (e.g. whether you panic or suffer from anxiety)

— Hormone surges and related physical changes in your brain/body

— How you manage stress (e.g. whether you have a glass of wine, eat, go out for a walk, meditate, smoke, etc.)

And while we're talking about anxiety, it's important to think about how it can affect our physical health and consider its cumulative effect. If you suffer from anxiety or have ever felt anxious, you will know how all-consuming it can be. I am sorry you've had to endure that awfulness. Take that anxiety up a level and you've got a full-blown panic attack, an entirely horrible occurrence that happens to many, many good people.

I had my first panic attack in the middle of a busy market and had no idea what was happening to me. Two of my kids were with me at the time and I managed to find somewhere for us all to sit down as I felt the world blur around me. Swamped by confusing feelings and physical responses, I sat quietly with my bewildered boys until their dad returned from the cheese stall and I promptly burst into tears.

If you have ever felt like that, then know that you are not alone and I know how blinking awful it is.

As I touched on earlier, when we are anxious, scared or panicked, our 'fight or flight' response can kick in. This is the ancient reflex that was cleverly designed to turn on our stress hormones, such as cortisol and adrenaline, and encourage us to flee to safety if, say, a woolly mammoth was chasing us down the street. Excellent for prehistoric times, but less so now. Now, if you are an anxious type, your fight or flight may be activating willy-nilly, flooding your body with stress hormones that it doesn't really need and can have trouble getting rid of.

What does it feel like when this is happening? Well, it can happen very quickly and the first you'll know of it are things like a pounding heart, breathlessness and feeling pretty sweaty. These delightful symptoms are turned on by those helpful stress hormones.

And just say you are one of those anxious types, what happens when stress hormones stay in your body? According to a 2011 article from the good folk at Harvard Health Publishing, 'Understanding the stress response', these surges 'can damage blood vessels and arteries, increasing blood pressure and raising risk of heart attacks or strokes'. The Harvard researchers say that high cortisol levels are meant to help the body recover from a stress response, but they can also have other effects – like making us gain weight because our body thinks we need more energy to fight off the 'threat'. Cortisol will also tell our body to store the nutrients we don't use … as fat.

There are other downsides of all that cortisol. It can cause problems with learning and memory, lower bone density, increase the risk of depression and other mental illnesses, lower our immune function and reduce our life expectancy.

That's a lot of reasons to address the stress in your life and pay attention to the physical effects of mental ill health, isn't it?

If we can find ways to reduce the pressure we are under and also to feel more cared-for emotionally, we are much more likely to boost our overall health for the long term … and feel less like a damp sock in the bottom of the washing basket. It's a total win-win.

What do YOU need?

Thinking about what you need to feel your best can be confronting, even triggering. This is especially so if you've been angrily ruminating on this very subject for months or years as you've put everyone else's needs before your own. Perhaps you've even forgotten who you are and what you need, because you are so caught up in parenting and working and running a house and trying so very hard to make everything work brilliantly.

As you read through this book, know that there are lots of other women thinking about this very same thing. Let's do more than think about it, buddy! Let's sidestep that way of being and learn how to put our wellbeing right up there with our children's. In fact, let's put ourselves a few steps ahead.

So let's get started by figuring out some things you need right now.

Do you need:

To be listened to?

To be understood?

To get more sleep?

To see a counsellor?

To be a 'better parent'?

To get a job you like?

Some time off?

Someone to help you?

To care for your body more?

More friends?

To not have to think of every bloody thing?

To be cared about and thought of?

A partner? (Or a different partner?)

All these things and more?

THINK ABOUT WHAT YOU NEED

Grab a pen and start documenting what you need. Have the tissues on standby and go into as much detail as you can. It's okay to feel emotional as you sort through this stuff. In fact, it's normal. Sob on, my little peach.

The main aim here – apart from some possible crying – is to begin documenting these important things about … YOU!

•

Writing down what you most need and want gives you somewhere to begin, helps you to stay on track and makes your progress (and any missteps) much easier to see.

•

This list will also be really, really helpful when it comes to working out what to say when other people ask you, 'How can I help?'

What do I need?

Some ideas on how to ask for help

**Step 1:
Start small or big
– both are okay.
Just start.**

Perhaps you might find yourself asking a favourite mum at the school gate to take your child home one afternoon a week (and you do the same for her) to extend your kid-free day a little longer and deepen your friendship.

Perhaps you might find yourself chatting to another nice mum at swimming lessons and accidentally bursting into tears as you reveal how under pressure you feel, only to receive an offer to catch up away from all those drippy kiddos.

Perhaps you might catch the eye of the other yawning parent at the school concert and bail him or her up later to organise a debrief in the very near future.

Perhaps you might ask your favourite family member if they want to go on a special outing with you and the kid/s. It might give you some time to talk about what's going on for you.

Perhaps you might ask one of the other school mums who seems a bit like you to catch up for a cup of tea on the weekend.

If reading Step 1 has made you break into a cold sweat or want to burrow into a pile of cosy blankets, consider moving straight to Step 3.

Step 3:
Manage underlying mental health issues.

Step 2:
Wade in there for the long haul.

Sometimes we have an underlying health condition that makes asking for help or connecting socially feel pretty impossible. Conditions such as depression, anxiety and PTSD can all make connecting with other people really hard. If you feel this could be something that is stopping you from living the life you most wish for, your doctor and/or mental health professional can assist you.

Know that the friend or family connections you are making or strengthening now can last a lifetime. Every time you open yourself up to being helped, you are creating stronger bonds, sometimes even more so if you return the favour when you are able to. Letting people help you and helping them is a real investment into your future support network.

It's really very much worth taking a step towards treating the illness that is getting between you and a more connected, supported and friendly life. I have been in this position and seeking medical support helped me immensely and made being social and friendly much less difficult, so I'm confident it will provide some relief to others, too.

40 NON-WRONG THINGS TO SAY
TO A VERY TIRED MUM

Leave this page artfully ajar if you are a shy sort, or take
a photo of it and post it on social media if you are not!

1. I hope you don't mind but I just left a bottle of wine and a wheel of brie on your doorstep! Love you!

2. Can I borrow all your children for the afternoon?

3. Would you like me to come over so you can talk at me for an hour or so? It would be my total pleasure.

4. I've made too many freezer meals! I'll drop some off this morning – they have instructions on the containers.

5. Would you like me to bring your favourite wine and cheese over and help you bath and feed your kids, and read them bedtime stories?

6. If you let me fold your laundry, I'll let you be my extra best friend.

7. Yes. I will stay at your house overnight so you can go to a hotel and have some space/sleep/sassy times.

8. A lot of the time, being a mum is a bit shit, but no-one actually tells you that.

9. I was making soup and I thought that it was something your family would like, so I doubled it because that's just as easy.

10. Yes, relationships are bloody impossible sometimes. I'm here if you feel ready/able to talk about it.

11. Yes, children are bloody little buggers a lot of the time. Let's sit them in front of a movie and drink some wine in the kitchen.

12. Here is a house cleaner once a week for eight weeks. This is my gift to you.

13. I've just told your partner/mum/housemate that I'm surprising you with a night out *sans* kids! Be ready at 6! Dress casual! It's all organised! I'll pick you up!

14. Can I take your teenager out for coffee and a bit of a natter?

15. If you ever need help with ANYTHING, I am here. I'll drive you to the doctor or tag along anywhere if you are feeling uncertain. Not. A. Problem.

16. Can I come over and play with your kid for an hour or two while you do other stuff? I'll bring snacks!

17. Cereal really *can* be dinner, can't it?!

18. Can I get your shopping for you or mind the kids so you can shop alone?

19. You are a brilliant mum and you are doing a great job.

20. Of course it's okay to wear your PJs all day!

21. Yes, work/life balance is a myth and it's totally normal if you're finding it a juggle. Can I come over and make dinner for you all one night? I'll bring the ingredients *and* clean up!

22. It's hard. What you feel is normal and doesn't make you a shit mum!

23. You know that lovely little playgroup in the local hall? May I pick up your three-year-old every Monday morning and take him there?

24. How can I help? Nothing is out of bounds. Laundry? Cleaning? Changing bedding?

25. Yes, tell me all the horrible things your child has done today. Get it off your chest. (And yes, I know you still love them.)

26. I'm shouting you all chicken and chips tonight! I'll just drop and run. Do you prefer coleslaw or Greek salad?

27. Sometimes births don't go the way we thought they would and it's okay to be sad. It's traumatic and scary. You did so well and you are amazing.

28. Can I pick up your kids from after-school activities and take them out for dinner?

29. Hi! I'm here to grab your kids and take them on an adventure. I'll just pop the bath on for you and make your bed all cosy first, though. I'll give them dinner and bring them back after that.

30. Girls night out. Plus a sleepover at mine (no kids allowed). Let's just be us for a night.

31. Look at your daughter go! She is learning to dress herself, and summer dresses in the middle of winter are just the thing. Exactly what my daughter used to do.

32. I need a child to take to that new animated Disney film. Would you lend me yours? We'll be gone for four hours because I think milkshakes, fries and a movie debrief are a good idea for afterwards.

33. I'm heading to the park with my kids and thought I'd take yours, too. Enjoy the quiet!

34. Sorry to hear you are having a shit week. Parenting is basically learning how to take deep breaths. Let me take your kids for a few hours – I will come and pick them up, feed them and return them exhausted.

35. Do you need me to run any errands for you?

36. Ring the school and let them know I'll be picking up your kids.

37. I've been to the library and am now looking for some children to read twenty storybooks to. Are yours up for it? I will bring healthy snacks!

38. Can I spend some time with you and your kiddos? That way I can learn how to care for them and give you a break sometimes.

39. Here are some flowers/herbs/lemons from my garden to brighten your day.

40. Would you like to watch rubbish TV with me and enjoy this amazing bounty of takeaway food?

Where to find support if you are feeling under pressure and isolated

Talk to a trusted family member or friend about what you're going through.

And talk to your doctor. They are ready to listen and can help you connect to mental health support (more on this in Chapter 10). If you don't feel like you can talk to your doctor, ask around for suggestions on a more empathetic one. Online school mum groups or neighbourhood social media groups are a good place to do that.

SEEK ONLINE SUPPORT

Australia – Beyond Blue
beyondblue.org.au

UK – Heads Together
headstogether.org.uk

International – Better Help
betterhelp.com

GET HELP ON THE PHONE

Australia – Lifeline: 13 11 14

NZ – Lifeline: 0800 543 354

UK – Samaritans: 116 123

US – Lifeline: 1 800 273 8255

Canada – SAM: 1 866 277 3553
(outside Montreal) or
514 723 4000 (Montreal)

CHAPTER 2

YOU CAN DO THIS

When you're feeling overwhelmed

Living life, not just surviving

Very often when we're trying to live a happy and fulfilling life, all kinds of things keep getting in the way and making everything seem too hard. Let's talk about how you might be feeling and the sorts of things that might be making your life feel a bit like a parent-themed episode of *Survivor*.

Overscheduling, overwhelm and an overflowing list of hard things sitting on the backburner all diminish our quality of life, making us feel stuck and even a bit hopeless. Let's find some ways to sort out all those 'O' words and get things back on track.

Keeping days as simple as possible

It's easy to feel like your days are just for 'getting through' when you are trying to look after kids as well as yourself.

If you're very deep in the trenches of parenting, getting to the part of the day when you can put your head on your pillow might be your chief survival strategy. That is entirely understandable. Perhaps the notion of building goodness into your day might make you do one of those snarky sorts of laughs. It can feel impossible.

There are so many completely understandable reasons why life might be hard. Throw in a child (or two, or more) and it is no wonder that things constantly seem to be pear-shaped, perhaps making you ask yourself, 'What the heck have I done here and where has my life gone?'

You might be the mum who is:

Just so, so, so very tired

Dealing with partner issues

Caring for a child with a disability

Coping with your own disability

Parenting with little support

Dealing with mental health challenges

Managing a chronic health condition

Feeling super fragile

Parenting a super-challenging child

Finding parenting super challenging

Facing financial stresses

Or you might be a combination of several of these things.

Whatever your situation, it's important to note that you have every reason to be finding life bloody tricky. Life *is* tricky. Being a human in this complicated world is hard. Having a child is hard, having children is hard and life is often hard. Being in a relationship is hard. Not being in a relationship is also hard. Those are the bare-bones facts of it all.

BUT ... the good news is that you are not on your own in all this tricky stuff and there are lots of different strategies you can try, and people who can help you get things a bit more sorted when you feel ready.

One simple way you can start a cascade of positive consequences is to pare back some of the things you and your child are doing. Forget all that pressure to cram the days with stimulating stuff. Think about what you are not enjoying and what your child is not really into. Step back from those things and give yourself some extra time to do the things that matter most to you.

Those things that matter most could be anything, really. Perhaps it's something practical like planting your child in front of their favourite show while you sip a glass of wine, plan your week's meals, order all the groceries you'll need online and free yourself from those drama-filled supermarket runs.

— Perhaps it's cancelling your child's Saturday morning sport and switching it for a coffee and pastry-filled picnic in the park where you get to breathe a bit and your child gets to go nuts on the slide with plenty of *pain au chocolat* for fuel. Bonus points if you invite another mum friend and child along!

— Perhaps it's ditching chores some days and heading for the hills or the beach for a long walk and hot chips in the car on the way home.

— Perhaps it's forgoing this week's tutoring session for the latest instalment of your favourite movie franchise and a ridiculously giant box of popcorn.

— Perhaps it's switching swimming lessons for a giant kid bubble bath, with your child soaking up some fun tub time while you sit on the floor sipping something delicious and chatting to them about their day (and yours!).

I don't know what things you need to give up, but when you do give them up, think about what you could do to replace them. Slot in something super simple that benefits you, but also factors in keeping your child busy and happy. Clearly you don't want to swap one pesky thing for another.

While giving things up is a great strategy for easing the pressure of mum life, take into account that some of the things you are doing provide you with important connections to your community. Carefully weigh that up and if you have friendships that are specific to those activities, be sure to take them with you into the rest of your life. Grab phone numbers or social media details and follow those you've buddied up with on social media. You can get in touch later for a park date or a coffee catch-up or a sneaky glass of wine. (Do it! Get in touch!)

Being honest with your kids about your struggles

It seems so simple, but so many parents are not honest with their kids. If your child is driving you absolutely nuts, one of the best things you can do is sit down – at their level, if possible – and say, 'I'm not really feeling like a good mum right now. I'm not sure what I should be doing, but know that I love you and I'm going to work it out.'

One of the best mum tips I could ever give you is this:
Be honest with your kids about how you are feeling.

It alerts your child to the fact that you are a kind, caring, flawed human. Very, very often it completely diffuses whatever tricky situation is playing out.

Clearly, being honest does not mean saying, 'You are driving me up the wall, you little shit.' No, that will not help. Think more about a sort of core honesty, talking about what is truly happening for you at the heart of everything.

'I'm feeling
a bit overwhelmed
and am trying to work
out how to be a good
mum right now.'

'I'm worried
about you
and I want to find
a way to help
you.'

'I've had
such a hard day
and I'm trying to feel a
bit better so I can help
you to feel better. What
can we do to feel better
together?'

You can write your own 'script', of course, but think about how you can be honest and vulnerable and kind to yourself (and your child) in those challenging moments. You don't need to go into a lot of detail – burdening your child with too many worries will help neither you nor them. Keep it simple. Less is more. Be guided by my examples.

I realised very quickly that this was the best approach for me when it came to my kids. It felt a bit weird sidestepping the authoritarian-style parenting that had been modelled to me. But when I did, I realised that my kids still respected me in the wake of my 'I haven't got it all together' reveals and in fact they felt closer to me and perhaps trusted me more, too.

Let's face it, if you are caring for your child and things have turned upside down and you've started yelling at them, they probably know you don't have all the answers already. Approaching the parent–child gridlock from a more open and honest position has to be a better strategy than screaming red-faced with your hands on your hips. Again. Children are often astonished to hear that their parents struggle with life's challenges. When you reveal that you are having a hard time, they will often rally to support you, and whatever was going on quickly slips into the background.

This honesty is something you should be mindful of in all kinds of mum situations. Being vulnerable and honest is a strength. By modelling this behaviour you are teaching your child very important lessons about self-awareness, emotional regulation, compassion and feelings in general. You are also parenting them respectfully and giving both of you the opportunity to grow closer as you work things out together.

As a parent, you do not have to be the person with all the answers. What you do need to be is a kind, caring human who keeps your child well, feeling safe and loved.

Of course, it's not just your own feelings that matter in the parent–child relationship. Your child's feelings need to be respected and validated, too. So very many issues around problematic mental wellbeing in adults stem from not being listened to and understood as a child, and the struggles that creates as we try to become fully functioning adults.

As Philippa Perry (who is married to artist Grayson Perry) says in her book, *The Book You Wish Your Parents Had Read (and Your Children Will be Glad That You Did)*, parents need to be a 'container' of their child's feelings. This means witnessing your child's feeling, understanding that feeling, helping them to put the feeling into words and finding ways to help them express the feeling, while avoiding being overwhelmed by their behaviour/feeling or punishing them for it. (I am here to put up my hand as one of those parents who has been overwhelmed by their child's feelings! Argh.)

Noticing and understanding our children's feelings and comforting them as they deal with them is the other side of this vulnerability coin.

Positive parenting qualities

I wanted to find out what other people thought a good parent should embody, so I asked the people I know what qualities were most important in mums and dads. They said good parents are:

emotionally available
respectful
encouraging
resilient
reliable
accepting
motivated
unconditionally loving
honest
responsible
good listeners
empathetic
mindful of boundaries
compassionate
vulnerable
present
flexible
positive
trusting
kind
adventurous
patient
humorous
fiercely loving
interested
joyful
open-minded
independent
strong
non-judgemental
self-aware
calm

What. A. List. Let's call these qualities 'good parenting pillars'.

Clearly you don't have to incorporate all of these things at the same time as you parent – that would be near impossible. Do not try that at home! What you *should* take away from this list is that there are so many different positive ways to parent and that everyone's ideas are different.

Please know that nobody is hitting all these marks on any given day. No hecking way! Do not look at this list as a series of 'must-dos'. Rather, look at it as a list you can cherrypick from as needed or come back to for a bit of a reset if you're feeling like you've gone a little off track. It's also a pretty damn good guide to being a nice human being, so why not take it into your life and your other relationships as well?

Thinking more about the type of parent you want to be can help fine-tune your approach and give you something clear to aim for.

You could select three 'hoped for' parenting qualities and when you are struggling you can think about how to align with even just one of them. Or you could choose one to focus on each week and build up your positive parenting muscles incrementally.

Maybe your own most 'hoped for' parenting qualities aren't even on the list my buddies made. That's okay, too. You do you!

If you can't align with any of your parenting pillars and want to throw them in the bin because you're feeling too crappy? Head to page 128 for ideas on what to do next.

Remember how you wrote down the things you need (page 33)? Now it's time to write down what you want from your parenting. Turn over the page and write down your three parenting pillars. You can use the list on page 52 as a guide, or come up with your own.

What three parenting pillars
or qualities are important to me?

Dear Pip

'My life is very hard right now and I'm feeling like a terrible mum.'

Okay, you might be thinking, those positive parenting qualities are all well and good, but my life is very, very complicated at the moment and that's the last thing I can think about. Give. Me. A. Break.

I get it. I honestly do. You may be dealing with some big issues in your life right now and the stress you are going through may feel like it's spilling into all parts of your life. Building up your parenting self-esteem and modelling excellent parenting behaviour might seem impossible.

When my relationship finally unravelled I found myself broke, in debt, in a deep depression, fighting off panic attacks and generally feeling utterly hopeless and having what they used to call a nervous breakdown. I had a bunch of urgent and non-urgent circumstances that needed to be sorted. I was anxious, sleepless, ashamed and very, very sad. Perhaps you have felt some of this, too.

When I felt like this, I eventually (begrudgingly) realised that I had to take action because the complications felt like they were growing and feeding off one another like some sort of ugly monster. I had to save myself. I had to shake off the shame and fear and deal with the things that seemed too hard, because they felt like they were suffocating me and that is not a good situation in anyone's book. I had to be brave and start untangling the hard things that were keeping me awake at night. I figured that once I faced the tricky stuff, I could start building a much more nourishing and happy life. And I did just that.

I want you to know that if I can do it, you can do it. You truly can.

Let's break it into some manageable chunks.

The fix-it list: Sorting out the tough stuff

When life feels like a giant scramble of awfulness, I like to take a sheet of paper and start mapping out a plan of attack. The bigger the paper, the better, but just use what you've got. No need to head to the stationery store – the time is ripe to get started right now!

Begin with getting all those complications out of your head and onto a page in point form.

1. Write down every single complication that is making your life hard at the moment. Write them in different positions on the page. Mention it all.

2. Underneath each complication, write down what you need to do to make it LESS complicated, or better still what you need to do to make it go away. Let's call these complication 'to-dos'.

3. Some complications are linked to others, so draw arrows between linked complications.

4. Look at the to-dos. Which are most important to get things moving? Which rely on the input or support of others? Number them in order of priority.

5. Now get to work. Make a 'fix-it list' of the most important to-dos and start working on those each day.

6. You might need to discuss your to-dos with a partner or relative who will be affected. You might need to request support from a professional. Now is the time to do that. Do you need legal advice? Do you need financial advice? Do you need medical advice? Something else? Write that down next to the appropriate complication. Let's sort it all out.

Your fix-it list might seem daunting, your page (or pages!) full of complications might seem overwhelming, but I am here to tell you that beginning to get things sorted out is going to make you feel so much better. Worries and tasks that have been hanging over you, squishing stress into every part of your body (and possibly onto your child/children) seem way less scary when you look them in the face.

And guess what? The ones that don't feel less scary are the ones you can enlist even more help with. You can talk to a psychologist about finding ways to manage the scary bits. They will help you develop some strategies to process the big feelings you are having about those hard bits. More about that in Chapter 10.

Things you might need to work on

Let's drag it all out into the light of day and do a little bit of a status check.

It feels so much better (sometimes not immediately, but eventually!) to be clear about what you're working with, so you can move through and away from all that worry. Here are some things to put on your list. Take a deep breath, sip some tea (or wine) and be brave. You can do this.

'THINGS TO FIX' SUGGESTIONS

- Money issues
- Work issues
- Physical health issues
- Mental health issues
- School or childcare issues
- Housing issues
- Relationship issues
- Friendship issues
- Family issues
- Legal issues
- Bureaucratic issues
- Business issues

Ugh. Monster things. Get them all out and down on paper so you can start sorting this out and feel lighter and free-er and much more like yourself.

Underneath your fix-it list, write: I can do this. Write it more than once if that helps. You *can* sort this stuff out and shake off at least *some* of the worry and stress you are living with.

I have used this method myself to brain dump a bunch of horrible stuff into the light of day, where I then began chipping away at these long-tucked-away and stressful to-dos. It made me feel so much better to have all of those things out of my head. I was able to sleep better, it dialled down my anxiety a little and it made me feel strong.

— I was strong enough to look my difficulties in the eyes.

— I was strong enough to find ways to sort out the hard things.

— I was strong enough to look after myself by being pragmatic and proactive.

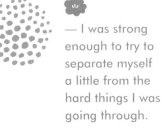

— I was strong enough to try to separate myself a little from the hard things I was going through.

— I was strong enough to figure out a way to give myself some respite.

And I am sure that YOU are strong enough, too. You are. Plus? You have me in your corner!

Once you begin to address these underlying complications, you can begin to care for yourself more wholeheartedly — perhaps to even begin to feel better about your life and your precious family. Perhaps to even begin to notice those excellent parenting qualities that you thought you were too messed up to be displaying.

I am positive that this is the case. You just need to make some moves towards untying some of those complex life knots. I am so sure that you can slowly, slowly begin to sort out all of the crappy stuff and feel more like yourself.

How do you talk to yourself?

Are you shifting uncomfortably in your seat as you read that question? I guarantee you are not the only one. Negative self-talk is an omnipresent downer for many of us. Unforgotten words seep back in from childhood, flooding in from the meanest and most bewildering parts of ourselves. They may tell us we are all kinds of awful things, sap our confidence, make us tired and generally extract the joy from life. Luckily, it doesn't have to be that way.

Because we are clearly in a 'sorting it all out' sort of mood, now is the time to think more about the way you talk to yourself, be it in your head or by forming actual out-loud words.

Know that this sort of intrusive, nasty self-chatter is getting you nowhere. Also? It's not true. Further? It's impacting on your child and the way they look at the world, whether you realise it or not. Children are clever and they pick up on the things that we think we are hiding from them. Your self-judgement may transform into their own self-judgement. Or it may teach them to be judgemental of others out there in the world. Clearly that's not what you're going for, so let's wipe the slate clean and start again.

Treating yourself as kindly as you would a dear friend is one simple way to reset that self-talk and make it much more positive. If you wouldn't say it to a dear friend, then don't say it to yourself. Simple, *non*?

There are lots of other ways to redirect negative inner chatter and quieten the mean voice in your head. When you catch yourself cycling negative thoughts, ask yourself a few simple questions to shake out that snark. You could try:

Are my thoughts based on facts or feelings? Are they truth?

Will this matter a week from now? Or a year from now?

Is there another way to think about this?

Am I catastrophising? (More on this on page 180.)

Is this thought helping me to live the life I want to live?

Good morning, feelings!

Another excellent strategy for dealing with negative thoughts is to begin every day talking to yourself in a kind and caring manner. Get up, wash your face, look in the mirror and ask yourself: 'How am I REALLY feeling today?'

Here is a list of feelings that you might be experiencing. Pick one or two that match you and your mood. Then, with that in mind, think about what you need to do to take care of yourself.

HOW ARE YOU FEELING TODAY?

insecure	vigilant	sad	threatened
self-conscious	hopeful	devastated	scared
unsure	optimistic	neglected	frightened
shy	confident	abandoned	nervous
introverted	positive	sorrowful	resentful
happy	loving	depressed	panicky
joyful	tender	miserable	intimidated
pleased	warm	heartbroken	alarmed
delighted	mad	hurt	anxious
carefree	suspicious	angry	startled
buoyant	cynical	frustrated	unsafe
jealous	sceptical	annoyed	affectionate
protective	dubious	irritated	worried
	lonely	furious	

Once you've settled on how you're feeling, it's time to plan your day accordingly. The idea is to make adjustments that work with your life's demands. Whether you have two minutes or two hours, be your own best friend and make your wellbeing a priority. Do you need to have a quieter day to address that bone-tiredness? Make a giant pot of soup to boost your mood? Check your child into after-school care so you can have a little bit of a breather? Take a long walk and sort out some clutter in your head? Meet a friend for coffee to salve that sadness? Book a doctor's appointment to sort out that health niggle? Work on your fix-it list? Have a cry in the shower? Snuggle up and watch *Bluey* with your child or *Gilmore Girls* with your teenager?

This self-awareness and self-compassion can help you to set the tone for the day, reminding you that you're not going to put up with that mean inner voice anymore.

Instead, you're going to circle back to that feeling and check in with yourself again. And make this a habit. Are you still feeling that way? How do you feel now? What small (or big!) thing can you do right now to address that feeling?

As you build this routine into your day, you'll find you feel a little better simply because you've taken the time to think about yourself. It feels good to make plans for your best day, taking into account how you are feeling and factoring that in among all the other busy to-dos. It feels good to look after yourself.

Feeling cared-for and prioritised is not the only benefit of this self check-in. Your revitalised 'feelings awareness' will also help you be more aware of and understanding of your child's feelings. Before you know it, you'll be a feelings boss, prioritising your own wellbeing and teaching your child important lessons about emotions and how to manage them.

Um ... No.

If you are finding that you aren't able to take the steps you would like to care for yourself properly, fear not. Flip to Chapter 10 to find out more about getting some extra support.

Very often when our mental and/or physical health is not optimal, this sort of self-compassion and self-kindness can feel impossible. You are not alone in that feeling and there are good people waiting in the wings to help. Know that you will not always feel this way and that things can get better – often astonishingly quickly – with the right support.

CHAPTER 3

CHANGING YOUR EXPECTATIONS

*When you're drowning
in mum guilt*

It's not just you

Guilt. Ugh. If you are a parent, it's highly likely that you have navigated the feelings of regret and responsibility that guilt embodies. They're heavy burdens to carry, making us feel sad, 'not good enough' and a bit hopeless, at times. Guilt dulls our sparkle and weighs us down.

If you are battling with mum guilt, you are not alone. According to a 2017 article in the UK's *The Telegraph*, nearly 90 per cent of mothers feel guilty at some point and 21 per cent feel this guilt all or most of the time.

Those figures seem surprisingly low to me. Guilt is part and parcel of mum life, and it can shapeshift into feelings of shame if we let it. So let's not. Being open and honest about guilt can help to shake up the stigma and shake off the shame.

Mums feel guilty for all sorts of reasons. We're amazingly clever at finding things to feel guilty about, in fact. Perhaps it's things you've said to your child. It might be things you've done. You might feel guilty about opportunities you can or can't give your child. And don't even get me started on the feeding of kids!

So, what do we do about all this guilt?

Experts tell us that it can be really helpful to reframe our mum guilt and consider what it might be signalling. It could be signalling that you are overwhelmed and need to pay some attention to yourself and your scheduling. Or that a particular routine or activity is not working out for your family and needs a rethink. It could be that your expectations of yourself or your child are way too high and need adjusting. It could be a sign that you need to research some new strategies for dealing with your child's behaviour.

If you flag this guilty feeling as a 'message' rather than a signal of failure, you can work on moving past it in a constructive way. It's a much better approach than ruminating on the (false) conclusion that you are the worst mum ever.

Adjusting to being a mum is HARD and we don't talk about it enough

Have you ever wondered why there are so many books about caring for babies, children and teenagers, but so few books about caring for mums? I have, clearly, because I am writing this book and it makes me angry that mums are not the focus of more research and attention. Becoming a mother is a huge transition and yet the focus is always on the best ways to look after the children we birth. No wonder mums are dealing with confusing feelings like guilt, shame and disappointment.

Anthropologist Dana Raphael picked up on this problem way back in 1973. Dana was the first researcher to champion (and coin the term) 'matrescence', the changes a woman goes through when she becomes a mum. Researchers and writers such as Aurélie Athan, Alexandra Sacks and Amy Taylor-Kabbaz have continued to champion Dana's work.

What is matrescence?

Matrescence, named as a sort of maternal adolescence, describes the physical and emotional changes that a woman goes through when she becomes a mother. Chatter about matrescence is often focused around the early months and years, but feelings about motherhood's challenges can arise long after that because children and the challenges they bring are always changing.

Matrescence might prompt feelings and thoughts such as:

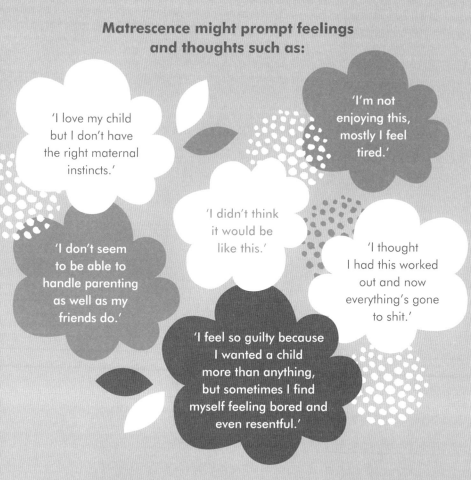

'I love my child but I don't have the right maternal instincts.'

'I'm not enjoying this, mostly I feel tired.'

'I didn't think it would be like this.'

'I thought I had this worked out and now everything's gone to shit.'

'I don't seem to be able to handle parenting as well as my friends do.'

'I feel so guilty because I wanted a child more than anything, but sometimes I find myself feeling bored and even resentful.'

You probably remember this huge adjustment when you first became a mum. It's a total shock to the system (and lovely at times, too!). But perhaps you haven't thought much about what's going on behind the scenes.

In her very popular TED Talk about matrescence, Alexandra Sacks explains the shifts that are occurring. She notes that when a child is born, a mother's body is flooded with the bonding hormone, oxytocin.

This helps you become attached to your baby, but at the same time a lot of other messaging is happening. You're being pulled to feed your baby, but you're also still wanting to do all the normal things like feed yourself, sleep, pee, spend time with your friends and family, learn and exercise.

Alexandra describes the way that many new mums find themselves feeling like they are in an 'emotional tug of war' as they try to figure out how to care for themselves and their baby's needs at the same time. 'If women understood the natural progression of matrescence,' she explains, 'if they knew that most people found it hard to live inside this push and pull, if they knew that under these circumstances, ambivalence was normal and nothing to be ashamed of, they would feel less alone, they would feel less stigmatised.'

Alexandra's remedy for this bumpy ride into matrescence? Talking more about it, being more open about what mum life is really like, and shifting expectations of what it means and what it feels like to be a parent, whether that's to a very fresh human or a teenage one.

The children make the mother

In a 2013 paper entitled 'Motherhood as Opportunity to Learn Spiritual Values: Experiences and Insights of New Mothers', Aurélie Athan and her colleague Lisa Miller delved deeper into this transformation to motherhood and highlighted some of the amazing and positive shifts that matrescence can bring. They hat-tipped the work of sociologist Martha McMahon, who discovered that for many women motherhood can feel like an 'essence-making' process that helps them settle on and discover who they really are and what they are truly capable of.

This view suggests that the child makes the mother (rather than the mother making the child!). 'From this standpoint, children are also empowered, as they carry the symbolic and real power to transform their mothers,' Athan and Miller explain.

I blinking love the idea of the child making the mother and have most definitely found it to be true in my life with my own children. They've taught me so much about myself and grateful feelings about their transformative powers have endured (unlike that long-forgotten school years mum guilt!).

The idea that the child makes the mother is also helpful when you're feeling like you've messed things up and should be doing a better job. Your child's job is to grow and learn. And guess what? Your job as a mum is to grown and learn, too.

You don't have to know it all or get it right every time. Next time you feel a bit wobbly, remember – this is one of those times your child is making you a mum! Lean in and learn more. It's a much better approach than feeling guilty or berating yourself.

The experience of unconditional love

Athan and Miller also explained that lots of mothers found having a child was their first true exposure to 'unconditional love' and the first time they felt beautifully and helplessly connected to another human. 'Some mothers compared their understanding of unconditional love to a journey, an ongoing process of refinement whereby their children continually drew them into greater intimacy, acceptance, and trust,' they wrote.

This was especially meaningful for women who had previously not let themselves love too deeply prior to motherhood, for fear of getting hurt. They were having their first big, deep feelings of love, thanks to their child. Mums described this love as 'life changing', 'overflowing' and 'at a different level'.

Let's talk about how hard it is

Those beautiful, challenging and vulnerable feelings are yet more of the difficult feelings we need to speak more openly about. And yet we don't.

It's hard to be vulnerable. Somehow it feels harder when you're a mum. If we admit our perceived failings, people will know that we don't have it all together. They'll ask us why we had kids in the first place. They'll keep a watchful eye on us from that moment forward. They'll take away our child and give her to a 'proper' parent.

Brené Brown, researcher and author of *The Gifts of Imperfect Parenting*, has some really interesting ideas about this sort of worst-case-scenario thinking. She calls it 'dress-rehearsing tragedy' and she notes that this reluctance to open up does us no favours. Brené says that 'to love is to be vulnerable' and to be vulnerable is to face 'uncertainty, risk and emotional exposure'.

You're probably reading this right now and thinking that sounds like nearly every blinking day of parenting and you, my dear reader, are not wrong. As Brené stated in 'The Wholehearted Parenting Manifesto', published on the *Huffpost* blog, 'Parenting is a shame and judgment minefield precisely because most of us are wading through uncertainty and self-doubt when it comes to raising our children.'

But parenting can also be a sort of masterclass in vulnerability, a masterclass that can help us to live more wholly in all the different areas of our lives, parenting-related or not.

Let's take a leaf out of Brené's book and aim to be vulnerable and true to ourselves, to ask for what we need, talk about our feelings, allow ourselves mistakes and take time to make amends. These are the sorts of life lessons our kids need most and they define good parenting and good living. Isn't that reassuring? Making mistakes (and making up for your mistakes) and being yourself are part of what it means to be a good parent!

Our expectations of mum life

I had my first child when I was very young, so I didn't really understand what was to come (and honestly, who does?). Everything I knew about parenting I'd gleaned from TV or from my own family. I knew I wanted to be a good parent and I definitely fell straight into the trap of trying to be a perfect one. Elaborate craft projects, home-made clothing, wholesome snacks, hours of story time, years of classroom volunteering – nothing was too good for my child!

It turns out I wasn't the only one chasing this 'perfect parent' dream (more on this on page 78).

Sociologist Martha McMahon has done a truckload of research into the difficult feelings that mums encounter throughout parenthood. One of the things she discovered after countless interviews with women is that they very often try to replicate a romanticised image of motherhood, and their valiant efforts to live out this 'perfect mum' role make them feel even more under pressure, overwhelmed and exhausted.

Thanks to social media, these idealised visions of parenting loom larger than ever. They are often the first thing we look at on our phones each day as we scroll through our Instagram or Facebook feeds. We notice the things that other parents are doing with their children or how neatly styled the highlight reel of their life is. We may even consciously or unconsciously aim to incorporate at least some of what we see into our own lives.

The problem is, we already have SO MUCH ON OUR PLATES. Adding even more to our to-do lists is a little bit nuts, right? A much better idea would be to simplify and clarify an achievable vision of mum life. If you dial back your expectations, you can hopefully dial back some of the parenting pressure and, in turn, feel more successful. This is a way of being kind to yourself and kind to other mums, too. Imagine their relief when they see you modelling a non-competitive and relaxed approach to parenting. They may even join you in stepping off the 'perfect parent' ride. You might even become firm friends!

As you grapple with guilt, perhaps it will help to know that you are not alone in those feelings of not being able to do it 'right'. I chatted to the mums I know and they spoke of the big divide between their real lives and the lives some parents on Instagram seemed to be living.

It's not just the examples of perfect parenting that can diminish mum morale. The public shaming of parents – both high profile and non-famous – is a reminder that if you don't stick to the rules, someone will be more than happy to call you out.

Author and TV presenter Chrissy Teigen is constantly judged for her parenting on social media, with nasty types chasing her off Twitter in 2020 by shaming her for not conceiving her children naturally. Chrissy and her husband John Legend's kids were conceived via IVF.

Beauty company founder and model Jennifer Hawkins dared to photograph her baby daughter without a hat on a sunny day (the hat was popped on straight after the photo) and her comments section speedily filled up with nasty snarks about her parenting. Sigh.

Singer Pink shared a photograph of herself cooking with her children and she was instantly shamed for apparently putting them in danger by letting them into the kitchen … because flames, knives, that sort of thing. Sigh.

The Bachelor alum and new parents Matty J and Laura Byrne were shamed for cuddling their newborn in the (empty) outdoor smoking area of a popular Sydney restaurant.

Even Meghan and Harry copped a dose of shaming when poor Meg was alleged to have been holding baby Archie the wrong way. Meghan was also judged for acting 'too pregnant'.

I could give a thousand more examples of this sort of public shaming of parents who were just trying to do the best for their families ... or simply having a relaxed moment when they didn't concentrate on getting everything right.

When we see this shaming behaviour online, we absorb it. We begin to feel like people are watching. We start to fear being the mum at the focus of this sort of chatter. We become anxious and second-guess our choices, never letting ourselves off the hook lest the parent police be lurking, ready to shame us and tell all their judgey friends.

We try to think of everything and do it all perfectly, just in case we become the mum who's judged to be doing it wrong (while trying so very hard to do it right!).

It's a wound-up way of parenting, but thankfully there is a much better way – a way that you might not have considered. While you'd be forgiven for thinking that most modern mothers seem to fall into the wildly oppositional 'don't give an eff mama' or 'perfect blessed mama' camps (particularly if your research was centred on Instagram), there are even more nuanced ways to look after your kids and be a mum. Who knew?!

'I see so many Instagrammers with kids and tidy houses and wish I was one of those.'
– **Rachel**

'I find it all so stressful and unachievable. Homes with zero mess, clutter or a speck of dirt. How is that even possible? Kids dressed in clothing where one outfit costs as much as my yearly clothes shopping budget. Lunch boxes filled with home-made friggin' pita chips (who does that for their kids?) and home-made guacamole. Little love cards popped in every day … Makes me laugh while also feeling like a failure.'
– **Janina**

'I don't follow any other mums as I find it too difficult mental-healthwise. I used to when my son was a baby and the pressure was too much for me.'
– **Rabia**

'All these mums of six kids who still look ripped as and run a successful business (supposedly). How?! All I can hope is my kids have clothes on, that I don't eat a whole fridge load of chocolate and that I remember to cook dinner.'
– **Belinda**

'I look at them very much aware that they're not real, that it's only a tiny snippet of their lives and it's impossible to be perfect like that! At the same time I wish I was super fit with a spotless house!'
– **Meaghan**

Why it's important NOT to be a perfect parent

Thankfully, there are lots of reasons NOT to be a perfect parent, so take that, judgey types!

In fact, many experts want you to know that being mindfully 'good enough' is a much better approach. Take British paediatrician and psychoanalyst Donald Winnicott, for instance. He began to champion the benefits of being a 'good enough' parent in the early 1950s.

Clearly this is at odds with the current enthusiasm for super-hands-on, best-of-the-best 'intensive parenting', which leaves many parents feeling like they are falling short and many kids finding it difficult to navigate life without mum or dad weighing in.

Perhaps you are one of these parents, trying to cater to all your child's needs, provide them with every opportunity, play with them in entertaining and engaging ways, all while hoping for three minutes to yourself to brush your godforsaken teeth?

Bonnie Compton is an American child and adolescent therapist as well as the author of *Mothering with Courage.* In a 2019 *Parents* magazine article, she explained how intensive parenting, where parents fear that they won't be able to give their kids the best opportunities or the perfect childhood, can lead to fear-based parenting. 'Their identity is tied up in their ability to parent,' she said. 'They fear that their child's success and behavior is reflective of how well they were parented.'

This is not a good situation for anyone. If you've found yourself trapped in this parenting perfection quest ... hugs to you. Obviously every parent does what they think is best at the time. Luckily, we can shift our approach whenever we feel ready.

Predating intensive parenting's impossible standards, Donald Winnicott had other much more achievable, healthy and reasonable ideas. He suggested that while our children are babies, it's important to respond to them as attentively as we can, because this helps them feel safe and form healthy attachments to their parent/s or carers. However, if we continue this level of extreme attentiveness in later childhood, we're teaching children that they are the centre of the universe and sabotaging their independence and resilience.

Accommodation: how much is too much?

Accommodation describes the way a parent 'softens' a child's life to take into account their fears and anxiety. This can confirm and even escalate the fears (even though this practice appears to make life more manageable in the short term).

Some of these parental accommodating habits might include outrageously complicated bedtime rituals, co-sleeping when you don't want to or pandering to particular routines that are inconvenient and stressful for you. When these sorts of behaviours set in, it's time to seek help, not surrender more of yourself and your time to your child. Constantly accommodating kids' needs in order to keep the peace is not only a pretty hefty burden for a parent to bear, it's also been shown to increase childhood anxiety.

In a 2020 article in *The Atlantic,* 'What Happened to American Childhood?', writer Kate Julian suggested that the majority of parents of anxious children find themselves engaging in accommodating behaviour to keep the peace. 'The everyday efforts we make to prevent kids' distress – minimizing things that worry them or scare them, assisting with difficult tasks rather than letting them struggle – may not help them manage it in the long term,' Kate pointed out.

If you needed permission to NOT pander to your child's every urging, this is it.

If your kiddo's demands are proving to be terribly prescriptive and are overwhelming you, it's important to seek support and set both you and your child up for future success – and better behavioural habits … for both of you!

It's much better to be a 'good enough' mother and to teach your child how to live in a challenging world by encouraging independence and even watching them fail a li'l bit sometimes. Guiding children through both the highs and the lows of life helps them to be better prepared for a world that won't always be on their side (even though clearly they are adorable and clever and just darling!).

'Good enough' parenting encourages compassionate and responsive care of a child, while also allowing them to experience difficulty and frustration when they're able to tolerate it. This style of parenting stresses that it's okay if things don't always go your child's way and you don't have to add to your own worries by buffering their path through life.

This 'good enough' approach is further proof that you don't always have to soften life's path for your child or parent them perfectly. Those bumps in the road build character and provide opportunities for your child to test their mettle. No need to feel guilty about that!

Dear Pip

'Sometimes I feel so angry!'

It's not unusual to get angry or frustrated with children, but for mums this is often seen as a failure. After an outburst you might feel regretful, ashamed or guilty. But it's important to note that anger and frustration are a normal part of parenting. We've been conditioned to see them as a defeat, but it's pretty impossible to parent a child without getting pissed off now and then.

When women become mothers, passing through this matrescence transformation, they find themselves in an institution that dictates that they should be able to adapt, that they should become more selfless, that they will direct only lovely feelings at their child, that they will keep it all together (and possibly manage a successful relationship with a partner, too).

But it simply doesn't work this way. It takes time to adapt, we often fall short of our expectations of ourselves, we struggle to balance nurturing ourselves and our children, we sob into our cornflakes. Because it's really, really hard to parent well and it's hard to be in a relationship, let alone 'take care of yourself'.

It's no wonder that some days erupt into tears and yelling. It's sad that this is so very often followed by feelings of disappointment in ourselves and a truckload of guilt. Getting angry is part of the normal range of emotions we all feel … even if we are mothers.

The poet Adrienne Rich wrote about this in *Of Woman Born: Motherhood as Experience and Institution.* She told of the guilt (there it is again!) that she felt when her children witnessed her anger, worrying that she was setting a poor example and that anger was a 'defect'. Thankfully it didn't take her long to realise that the ideal of a placid, constant, selfless mother was impossible to live up to.

Adrienne wrote this back in 1976, but many of us are still buying into the idea that anger somehow diminishes love, and that displaying anger is the defect that she writes of. It's not. It's normal. Mothers are human and sometimes things just get too much ... and they get angry.

Spending time feeling guilty about this is understandable, but it's important to give yourself permission to note your regret, then move on.

WHAT TO DO WHEN YOU'RE RACKED WITH MUM GUILT

1. Talk through what happened with someone else – these feelings are a normal part of parenthood and you don't need to feel ashamed.

2. Think about how you'd judge your best friend if she was in your situation. Offer yourself the same kindness.

3. Think about the facts and feelings of the situation. If you are telling yourself you 'should' have done something else, consider why you feel this way and if it's based on fact.

4. Write about what happened and what you might do differently next time.

5. Accept what happened – say, 'I did the best I could at that time' – and push on. Repeat that phrase if you keep ruminating on the cause of your guilt.

6. If you very often find that your guilt is swirling, it can be a great idea to talk to a counsellor about your feelings. Head to Chapter 10 for more information about seeking support.

CHAPTER 4

THE LONG GAME

*When you need a reminder
of the magic you're making*

Expect a few bumps in the road

Very, very often as my children were growing up, I would lie in bed going over what had happened that day and feeling terrible about perceived mistakes or lapses. Tears would run from my eyes to my ears and onto the pillow and I'd berate myself for being a shithouse mum.

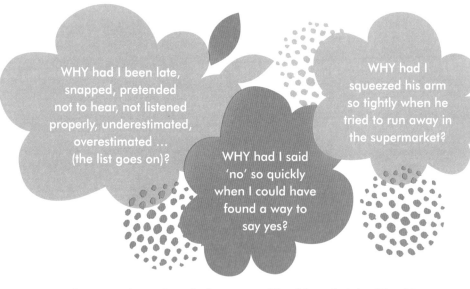

WHY had I been late, snapped, pretended not to hear, not listened properly, underestimated, overestimated … (the list goes on)?

WHY had I said 'no' so quickly when I could have found a way to say yes?

WHY had I squeezed his arm so tightly when he tried to run away in the supermarket?

I am certain you have had moments like this and nights like this, wearily staring into the darkness and trying to drift off to sleep as your supposed parenting errors play over in your mind.

It's a brilliant idea in these moments to think about the long game. Yes, today might not have gone the way you'd hoped with your kiddo, but think about your long-term relationship with your child and how you are nurturing that.

Every single parent in the history of parents slips up, has crappy days and feels too tired for the job at hand. But these bumps in the road are part of a much bigger parenting landscape, a landscape that's surrounding your child with a wealth of experiences and includes not just you but other family members, friends, people who care for and teach your child, people in their childcare and school community … and people they are yet to meet.

Your bumpy day with your child is just that. In fact, for many parents it's probably not even a bumpy DAY. It's likely a bumpy hour or a bumpy few hours.

NOTE: If every day is a bumpy day, there is support available and it's vital that families access it – for the wellbeing of parents and children. Turn to Chapter 10 for more about how to access help.

5 WAYS TO PUT PARENTING CHALLENGES INTO PERSPECTIVE

1. Observe the facts rather than judging or editorialising on them.
2. Try to avoid reacting with intense emotions – stay calm. Take a deep breath (or twelve).
3. Ask yourself how you will feel about this in a week, month or year.
4. Try not to catastrophise – just deal with what's actually happening right now, today.
5. Think about the overall long parenting game – what is your end goal?

What matters to kids?

Keeping a close eye on what you want for your long-term relationship with your child can help to bring the odd bumpy day into perspective. When you have days like these, know that these small dramas will not be what matters most to your child in the long term.

So what *is* most important?

A research review by UK charity The Joseph Rowntree Foundation found that a number of key parenting skills were important to kids' wellbeing. Security- and resilience-building behaviours included:

Warm, authoritative, caring
and responsive parenting

•

Open, participative communication
and problem-solving

•

Parenting with confidence
and flexibility.

It can be good to keep these overall goals in mind when things have gone a bit pear-shaped. Or flip back to the parenting goals you outlined in Chapter 2. Perhaps you'd like to update them with some of the above ideas.

Interestingly, it's not just the experts who are promoting these clear overall parenting approaches. Children are verbalising these important parenting skills, too.

Kids say that to be loved and cared for is what matters most. A 2007 report published by The Joseph Rowntree Foundation examined research about children's views of parenting. According to one 2000 study, most children said that parental love, emotional security and effective support were the most important things about being a family.

A 1998 study reported that children said they liked to be listened to, taken seriously and valued. A 2001 study found the same things. Kids also wanted to be consulted on day-to-day matters that affected them and their family, even if their parents made the final decisions. Kids valued strong relationships, love and support, and disliked family conflict. Family separation is manageable if they felt cared for, the research says.

THINKING ABOUT NEXT TIME

Rather than ruminating on the small dramas you've had with your child and feeling like the world's worst mum, think about the bigger picture. What was really happening?

1. What needs did YOU have that were not being met?

2. Are there ways you could approach this differently if a similar situation occurred again?

3. What needs did YOUR CHILD have that were not being met?

4. How did these contribute to the drama?

Treat yourself and your behaviour as a best friend would. Think it over, make a better plan for next time, give yourself a hug and move on.

Dear
Pip

'Will my kid remember that I lost it or was mean?'

When I asked my friends what they most remembered
about how their parents raised them, the answers
were really varied and interesting.

'I remember cooking after
school, my dad tucking me
in (numerous times because
I liked being tucked in
so tight I couldn't move),
reading, watching TV
together, my mum racing
home from work to cook
dinner, feeling safe.' **– Lexi**

'As I reflect back as an
adult, I see the way that
my mum instilled security
through routines and
predictability. We had
very little, and lived week
to week and through using
food banks.' **– Lisa Jane**

'We had some very trying
times, but mostly we were
at the mercy of how well
our parents knew themselves
and could manage their
own emotions, and to be
honest they didn't have
great training for that.'
– Caitlin

'I remember listening,
being given the benefit
of the doubt and being
driven around.' **– Kerri**

'I remember being ignored.'
– Catherine

'I remember the craft activities that our mum arranged for us. Spending family time together. Trips to visit grandmothers. Mum at tuckshop. Dad walking the little kids on his boots after work. Taking us camping, long bushwalks. There was a lot of farting and laughs.'
– **Angela**

'My beautiful mother would always build me up. Whenever I was upset, she would hold me very tight and tell me that I was smart, beautiful, talented and strong enough to withstand anything. She would do this when she said good night as well. I try to do that with my boys, too. I know some people would consider that coddling a kid, but it did so much to build my resilience.' – **Robyna**

'I remember terrible cooking, parties where adults were wasted, my mum sleeping a lot, moving house, road trips. Excellent music on vinyl. But mostly a lack of security.' – **Amber**

As you would expect, if kids do not feel loved, safe, secure, prioritised and/or cared for, they will take this into their adult life. We're not talking about the occasional mum stuff-up here – freaking out and yelling at your child every now and then is not likely to make a huge impact if they feel secure, prioritised, loved and cared for the rest of the time. These are all vital elements of a healthy childhood. It's when they are consistently lacking that the outcomes are really challenging for kids as future adults. So please don't beat yourself up about silly squabbles and slip-ups. Think big picture, reset and aim for a great parenting approach overall.

Let's look at those parenting skills again and aim for them as often as we can. It's not easy, but the payoff is unbeatable.

PARENTING SKILLS THAT KIDS AND EXPERTS RECOMMEND

Warm, authoritative, caring and responsive parenting

Open, participative communication and problem-solving

Parenting with confidence and flexibility

BOLSTERING PIKELETS
aka very tiny pancakes that make your worries go away (for a little while)

If in doubt … make pikelets! Pikelets are the stuff of childhood memories. If you're new to them, think very tiny pancakes and you're on the right track. They can be dinner or breakfast or elevenses and they can calm the most bonkers days. There is some magic at play in all that whisking out the lumps and pouring the batter and waiting for the bubbles to appear and sniffing that buttery, delicious smell. Not to mention the slathering with your favourite topping and the gobbling up.

When we were little, making pikelets was a sure sign that we were loved. They were always accompanied by cups of tea.

1 cup (150 g) self-raising flour
1 teaspoon baking powder
A pinch of salt
2 tablespoons sugar

1 egg
¾ cup (185 ml) milk
A dash of vanilla essence
Butter, for cooking

Sift the flour, baking powder and salt together in a large bowl. Stir in the sugar. Add the egg, milk and vanilla. Whisk until you have a thick, smooth batter.

Heat a heavy-based frying pan over medium heat. Brush the pan with a small amount of butter. Drop spoonfuls of the batter into the pan to create those very tiny pancakes. When bubbles appear on the surface of the pikelet, flip it over and cook the other side. Serve with golden syrup, butter, jam … whatever you fancy.

Makes 8

Work at being the calmest person in the room

If there is one piece of advice I can offer about being a parent, it's this: be the calmest person in the room. That is not to say that I have always abided by my advice, but there is something about having a parenting mantra that makes the whole mum thing less confusing.

'Be the calmest person in the room' is a good mantra to have.

It doesn't mean you are calm at all times. Nu-uh. But you can be calmer than your child and that's what counts.

Sometimes, when things get tough, you and your kiddo might begin to perform a kind of duet, taking turns at crying, throwing things, busting out full-body sobs and generally expressing extreme distress. One thing that might help you stop your own swirl into that undesirable performance is to remember that as the parent you need to at least try to be calmer than your child – no matter what age they are. Be they toddlers, kids or teenagers (even grown-up kids), they will appreciate your steady resolve and lack of freaking out.

It could be good to wear a badge that reminds you of this. You could even get a tattoo! I do not say this lightly because if there is one thing I know it's that children can often push you to be your worst self … and this mantra can helpfully nudge you back to the non-dark side.

Please know that if you and your child have recently been embroiled in a pair of complementary tantrums that left both of you breathless, this is quite normal. It can take a while to get the hang of the emotions and hoped-for outcomes that have you and said child bouncing some big feelings back and forth between you. But this little calmness mantra can remind you that: a) chucking the Nutella at the kitchen wall may not help (although it may!); and b) the circumstances may shift but you can still default to a trusty position – that of the calmest person in the room.

Today is as good a day as any to begin this calm-resetting strategy. It's not only going to be a positive for your child, who probably feels a bit wrongly done by when you keep yelling 'Why won't you listennnn to meeee?' or 'Go to beeddddddd!'. It also gives you a lifeline back to a different mum self. The one who (mostly) remembers to pull back and take some breaths before everyone's upset. And this sparks a much nicer feeling that hints at your frankly gobsmacking sensibleness in the face of someone who is clearly (temporarily) a little (or not-so-little) bloody monster.

This strategy doesn't only help with wrangling small and big children, it spills over into other areas of your life, too. Before you know it, you might have stopped yelling 'you bloody idiot' to people who can't merge lanes. You might even feel decidedly 'not annoyed' when someone cuts in front of you at the shops.

BUT, you may ask weakly, what happens if I was not calm? What happens if I did chuck the Nutella?

Well, I'm here to tell you that that is actually also okay. You've crossly stamped your feet where thousands of parents have trodden before you. Except maybe they stamped and threw a dish of gruel or a platter of Tudor-style peacock Kiev or a brontosaurus steak. You get the picture.

Rest assured that many brilliant parents have gone uncalmly before you. And tomorrow is a whole other day.

HOW TO BE THE CALMEST PERSON IN THE ROOM

Trying for a calmer default can help you feel way less crappy, feel like a much better mum and build stronger bonds with your child.

Remember, they're hurting, not *really* trying to hurt you.

Help your child manage their big feelings by noticing and naming them.

Share your calm – don't join their chaos.

Your child is in crisis, but YOU don't have to be.

Facing the long game together ...
with mindfulness

All that sharing your calm might seem a lot easier said than done, so let's sneak in a practical tip that can teach both you and your child emotional regulation, which can be really useful during tough times: mindfulness!

Part of this long-game thinking is about finding tools that arm you and your kids for a less stressful, more connected future, and mindfulness is one truly brilliant tool.

Mindfulness describes being present and completely engaged with what is happening in a particular moment. When we are practising mindfulness, we become aware of our thoughts and our feelings, and choose not to judge or distract ourselves in this moment.

Practising mindfulness can help you to become more aware of how you are feeling and less likely to rush headlong into chaotic feelings. Research has found that mindfulness can actually change the shape of our brains for the better, making us more predisposed to positive thoughts and emotions.

Teaching your child mindfulness? Great for the parenting long game, for both of you.

'Being a parent is an incredibly stressful experience in its own right,' David Gelles wrote in his 'Mindfulness for Children' piece in *The New York Times*. He explained that practising mindfulness with a child, even if it's only for a few minutes a day, can be a great way to teach these skills to your child, while looking after yourself at the same time. Win-win!

Many school-aged kids are already practising mindfulness via school programs, so this could be a great thing for your child to teach YOU more about!

PRACTISE 'S.T.O.P.' MINDFULNESS

This is an easy-to-remember, portable way to practise mindfulness, and one you can share with your school-aged child or teenager.

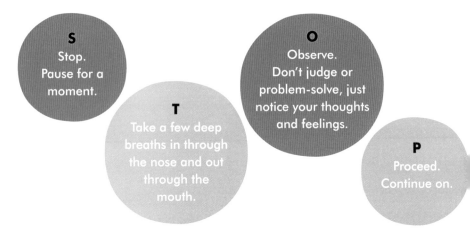

S
Stop.
Pause for a moment.

O
Observe.
Don't judge or problem-solve, just notice your thoughts and feelings.

T
Take a few deep breaths in through the nose and out through the mouth.

P
Proceed.
Continue on.

Mindfulness reminds us to be kind, compassionate and accepting of the moment we are in.

Long-game tips and tricks

This long-game thinking is an opportunity to shift your overall parenting perspective and there are a bunch of different strategies that can help you get closer to being the sort of mum you might want to be.

Everyone is different, but perhaps some of these ideas might help you to refresh your way of parenting (and make you feel much more positive about life in general!).

Let your face speak what's in your heart

In 2000, the late author Toni Morrison appeared on *The Oprah Winfrey Show* and shared a huge parenting lesson. 'When a kid walks in the room, your child or anybody else's child, does your face light up?', Toni asked a group of assembled women. 'That's what they're looking for,' she said.

Toni explained that when your child walks in and sees you checking their physical appearance, they don't interpret it as a demonstration of your love and care for them. They see your critical face and wonder what they've done wrong. She suggested that you should let your face show what's in your heart, and let your child see that you're glad to see them.

It's a tiny but powerful shift that can reset your day. And there's no time like today to begin doing this.

Try the 'I get to' switch

This may seem a little cheesy, but I promise it can help to change your approach, while also modelling excellent positivity and gratitude to (and for) your child.

When you catch yourself saying 'I have to', try switching it to 'I get to' instead.

'I have to take Sophie to soccer practice' becomes 'I get to take Sophie to soccer practice.'

'We have to go to the library' becomes 'We get to go to the library!'

'I have to read Jack a bedtime story' becomes 'I get to read Jack a bedtime story.'

'I have to pick up Max from his pal's house' becomes 'I get to pick up Max from his pal's house' (and also provides an excellent opportunity to chat in the car on the way home!).

It's an easy win, it boosts everyone's mood and it flips things brilliantly.

Approach motherhood as a growth exercise

Becoming a mum is a transformative experience and embracing this very steep learning curve with your L plates on can help to reframe any bumps in the road.

As author and psychotherapist Philippa Perry points out, a baby has never been a baby before. They're just learning! It's no wonder their behaviour is hard to predict. Parents are learning, too – parenting each individual child for the first time through all kinds of ages and stages. When you look at things from this point of view, it's not surprising that you can't rise effortlessly to every parenting challenge.

Every child is different and every day is different. Your child is learning and growing and taking leaps and sometimes retreating a few steps backwards. Your mum skills and responses might be doing the very same thing.

If you approach parenting from this 'learning on your feet' vantage point, it's a lot less demoralising when things don't go as expected or if you're unsure of what to do next.

Some mums also find that the big love they have for their child has sparked some big changes in how they feel about the world and their own lives. Becoming a mum has meant that their priorities have shifted and they're thinking differently about themselves and what's most important.

Research confirms that women may alter all kinds of life elements when they become a parent not just by necessity, but also because their attitudes shift. Health, relationships, living arrangements, financial plans and professional ambitions are often the first to get a mum-life shake-up.

Women report increased empathy and compassion. They also say that they become less self-centred. I know that I became far more curious, self-aware, environmentally aware, creative (more on that in Chapter 11) and caring. I became a better listener and more thoughtful in general, I think. I was also driven to cook more healthily, be a better role model, be better educated ... the list goes on.

I love this fresh idea of reframing parenthood as a period of growing and adapting, rather than a period of loss and/or mastery.

Granted, you probably are losing sleep, losing independence, losing money ... Many women find parenthood sparks mental and physical health concerns, or makes existing ones worse. There is no doubt that this is incredibly challenging. But there is goodness and growth in mum life, too.

The long game is not as long as you think

'Cherish every moment.' If there was ever a phrase that set parents' teeth on edge, it's that one, especially if you're parenting younger children. And especially if it comes via a well-intentioned older person who, you suspect, can't remember where they put their glasses, let alone what it's like to raise a kid.

Maybe you shuddered and wanted to throw this book as you read it? I get that. Parents who are being tortured on a daily basis by boundary-flexing, sleep-depriving, pouting, contrary thing-wanting children are not interested in any of that teary, nostalgic, magical motherhood nonsense. They have enough of their own welling-up to ponder, thank you very much. Maybe they have other people in their care who are constantly welling-up, even.

That said, I'm going in – flying in the face of the addled parents who don't need this nostalgic nonsense – because oh my gosh those truly *are* brilliant years. I'm proudly flying the flag for a very, very greedy amount of cherishing, when you can manage it.

Yep. That old lady at the supermarket talking to the yawning mum of small kids about how every day counts needs a high five because SHE IS ABSOLUTELY RIGHT. And, land sakes, imagine if we knew this – and I mean truly *knew* and *felt* this – when we were deep in the trenches of those years.

I'm *not* saying it would make everything rosier and magically inject a bracing dose of patience or resilience in parents who are fed up to the eye teeth with their child laughing in the face of screen-time limits or refusing to get out of bed and get dressed for school for the 127th time.

What I *am* saying is it might help a titch in those dark moments, and we should keep what these elders have to say in the backs of our minds.

What I *am* saying is … kids eventually leave.

I know that everyone *knows* they leave, in a sort of academic, hat-tipping, 'that's what we're working towards' way … But the leaving is beyond the knowing, because *knowing about* something is not actually feeling it or living it. It all seems good, in theory, but the fact is the knowing is not knowing, in this case.

Don't get me wrong, the leaving part is a bit brilliant, because … JOB DONE! TICK! (Well, sort of, because they will still dip in and out, scooping up love and a receptive ear when they need it.)

But the *leaving* bit is the end of the first major growing-up and wings-spreading and buggering-off part. And with that bit, you really *do* wave goodbye to things you didn't know you were going to miss – mess, for starters. There is less. It seems like that would feel good, but the juice-stained tabletop, rogue socks and unwanted crusts stuffed down the side of the couch weirdly feel like valid things to miss.

Noisy chatter and bingles
around the dinner table?
Missed.

A daily rhythm that includes a bunch of different
people's needs, all smooshed into a mashed-up life?
Missed.

The person who used to helpfully eat the leftovers and
fight the battle of food waste/tell you that pasta you
made the other night was brilliant?
Missed.

Even the person who left just enough milk for only
half a cup of coffee in the fridge?
Missed.

The person who used to bring their friends over
after school and play their music too loud and
slam siblings out of their room?
Missed. Missed. Missed.

Delving even further back, there are many miss-able things. There's no little hand extending up for reassurance or companionship as you wander down the street. No neck hugs. None, I tell you! There are no little voices delighting in things you had forgotten to notice: 'LOOK, Mum! A BUS STOP!'

There's no-one clammily crawling into your bed, annoyingly jumping on your bed or even casually *sitting* on your bed – you untying your shoelaces and thinking about whether the notes at the bottom of today's schoolbag will be crisp and dry or have the remains of a juice box seeping into them like an unwelcome tide, while they chat about some idiot kid at school who was rampaging through the classroom with a pot of glue and a bad attitude earlier that day.

Nope. The house is empty of them and their clutter and their clatter ... and their testing/lovely companionship.

As Gretchen Rubin, mother and author of *The Happiness Project*, reminds us, 'The days are long, but the years are short.'

CHAPTER 5

MUMS MATTER

MATTER

When you've forgotten who YOU are

Let's start with self-care

It's very, very easy to get lost in the frazzled world that is being a parent and to set aside your own needs ... and even your own true self. But we know that operating in 'survival mode' is not a terribly brilliant strategy, because as we neglect our hearts, minds and bodies in general, the body is keeping score. Your body knows exactly what's going on with you and, try as it might to keep you well, if you're not looking after yourself it will pull you up and sideline you, sooner or later.

It's time to begin building a healthier relationship with your whole self and to start finding time to not only practise some self-care on a regular basis, but also to take stock of what you really want and how you're going to edge in that direction.

Spending time away from your child

Having time away from your child or children is a blinking excellent way to recharge and get in touch with the non-kid things that matter to you most. That said, it's not that easy, is it?

Time out rarely feels achievable due to circumstances, logistics, guilt, someone screaming their head off and clinging tightly to you ... but if you can manage it, you won't know yourself afterwards. And your kids? Your kids will be thrilled with the much-happier parent who returns to hug them and tell them how missed they were.

SOME WAYS YOU COULD SPEND YOUR TIME AWAY

Perhaps it's overnight with someone you love

Perhaps it's a whole weekend away with buddies or your romantic interest

Perhaps it's just an hour or two to get your eyebrows sorted or hang out in your favourite bookshop

When my kids were toddlers, I'd time their morning nap to coincide with the moment that I wheeled their sleeping forms into my favourite cafe, sometimes walking them up and down the street until they finally dozed off. Then I'd spend 45 minutes or an hour drinking coffee and reading in peace. When they woke up, it was time to head back out into the world and I felt refreshed and happy to push on with mum life again.

Perhaps you have your own version of that waiting in the wings? Snuck in before work? On the way to kid pick-up? During soccer practice? Whatever you can manage, know that it's important and you deserve it.

If only we lived in a world where affordable and available child care was always easy to access, and where families and friends were ready and waiting to lend a hand. This is very often not the case, so here are some ways to shift your time and kids about to give yourself some much-needed (no doubt) 'me' time.

10 WAYS TO SNEAK IN SOME TIME FOR SELF-CARE

1. Make time! It's so hard, but it's so worth it.
2. Leave work 20 minutes early (take a shorter lunch break).
3. Get up 30 minutes earlier (sorry, but we do what we must to make things work!).
4. Take turns watching another mum's kids so you both can spend some time alone.
5. Meal plan and have your groceries delivered so you can utilise the time you save for yourself.
6. Encourage your children to help with chores so that it's not all falling on your shoulders and you free up some time.
7. Organise an hour or two of child care just so you can spend time looking after yourself.
8. Plan regular activities for your child that allow you a little bit of breathing space.
9. Lower your domestic standards and use the time you might have spent dusting to do something you love.
10. Take a day of your annual leave to do the things you love (without your kids!).

Sleep is queen

Sleep is vital for wellbeing, yet often wildly elusive if you are the parent of one or more children. Your sleep will be interrupted by all sorts of things if you are a mum. Children having bad dreams, night-wandering children, vomiting children, coughing children, sleep-talking children, hungry children, scared children. The list goes on. However, sleep is still absolutely worth prioritising if and when you are able to do so.

(If this seems impossible for you right now, I have lots of other ideas. Read on and know that one day, you will sleep again. I do it all the time now that my kids are older.)

10 WAYS TO PROMOTE SLEEP

1. Make your bed nicely each day and keep your bedroom tidy.

2. Have a very early night once a week.

3. Make 10pm your usual bedtime – it's when our stress hormone, cortisol, is at its lowest.

4. Avoid tea, coffee or other stimulants after lunchtime.

5. Be active each day, even if it's just a ten-minute walk to the bus stop.

6. Don't use your phone, watch TV or stream in bed – the blue light emitted from these devices sabotages sleep and inhibits the production of the sleepy hormone, melatonin.

7. Have a hot shower or bath before you go to bed.

8. Read yourself to sleep.

9. Try a white noise machine or app to help you doze off.

10. Keep your bedroom as dark as possible and consider using an eye mask.

Let there be light

I touched on light above, but it's important to note that exposure to the usual cycles of daylight and darkness is vital to our wellbeing, and worth thinking about when you are pondering self-care.

Our circadian rhythm is our inbuilt biological clock and it takes care of normal physiological cycles and processes. Circadian rhythm governs functions such as our core body temperature, sleep cycles, cell function and hormone secretion. When our circadian rhythm is out of sync due to lots of screen time, staying indoors or wakeful nights, our mood, metabolism and other functions are often out of sync, too.

If we ensure that we're getting plenty of time in natural light, we can optimise this natural rhythm and reap the rewards. This is stupidly simple self-care and we all need to opt into it as often as possible.

Feed yourself properly

Wander into any bookshop and you will find 238 zillion books on healthy eating. You could be forgiven for heading straight to the nearest cupcake shop and buying a baker's dozen in response to this confusing information glut.

However, it goes without saying that looking after yourself involves eating well at least some of the time. With this in mind, I've outlined three nourishing approaches to eating – Mediterranean, Japanese and Nordic. They're all backed up by science and don't have a single celebrity chef attached to them (as far as I know). Why not choose one of these cuisines, buy some ready-to-eat ingredients, arrange them on a board and call it a picnic plate? Lunch/dinner/whatever sorted!

PICK A FEEL-GOOD
EATING DESTINATION – OR MIX IT UP

Mediterranean

Plenty of: vegies, grains (mostly wholegrains), fruit, olive oil, beans, nuts, seeds, legumes, herbs and spices

Some: fish and other seafood
A bit of: chicken, eggs and dairy
A little: meats and sweets

Japanese

Plenty of: grains, vegetables, legumes, nuts and seeds

Some: meat and fish
A bit of: fruit and dairy
A little: sweets

Nordic

Plenty of: fruit, berries, vegetables, potatoes, legumes, wholegrains, nuts, seeds, rye bread, fish and other seafood, low-fat dairy, herbs, spices and canola oil

A bit of: game meats, free-range eggs, cheese and yoghurt
Very little of: other red meats and animal fats, and sweets

Connect to others

One of the most rewarding things we can do is to establish strong connections to family, friends and community. These links to others make us feel happy, secure and supported, giving our lives meaning and purpose. Fostering friendships and family bonds helps to maintain optimal mental and physical health, and can protect us from depression and anxiety.

What this means is that you should never, EVER feel that time spent with others is frivolous or unproductive. Every minute you spend with your friends or family is time spent putting some wellbeing bucks in the bank.

Call a friend and book in a coffee catch-up this instant! And if you can't catch up in person? There's no time like the present for a video chat. Put the kettle on and hop to it.

Spend time in nature

One of the easiest and best ways to look after yourself is to go outside and head for the nearest park for twenty minutes or so. Even just a short burst of time surrounded by nature can help to boost your wellbeing, whether you sit or walk or run or play.

The natural world has a way of taking us back to secure feelings we experienced playing outside as a child. It turns out there are lots of other benefits to being outdoors, too. Being in green spaces can improve mood, lower blood pressure, reduce stress hormone levels, boost self-esteem, reduce anxiety, enhance immunity and much, much more. Being outside relaxes us, makes us feel less isolated and promotes mindfulness and attention.

A recent study by the University of Exeter's European Centre for Environment & Human Health found that we should be aiming to spend 120 minutes a week in nature. People who did this were much more likely to report good health and psychological wellbeing than those who did not seek out green spaces. And it doesn't have to be all in one go – just eighteen minutes a day will pay dividends in terms of how you feel.

Another study, from The University of British Columbia, found that people who took a photo of the natural things they encountered in their day, and wrote a short note about how they felt about it, lifted their mood, making them happier. Perhaps this is why we see so many photos of pretty flowers and lovely, leafy limbs on Instagram – it's a proven self-care method.

If you are looking for a go-to way to take care of yourself, being in nature is an easy and free strategy.

Get out in a garden

Sue Stuart-Smith, psychiatrist, psychotherapist and author of *The Well-Gardened Mind*, wrote a whole book about the benefits of gardening and I think growing things is a brilliantly left-field form of self-care. Growing things brings together life's emotional, physical, social and spiritual aspects while improving fitness, mood and self-esteem. All that and you might end up with a bunch of basil or a bag full of cherry tomatoes … or a lettuce!

Why wouldn't you approach gardening as a self-care strategy?!

We know that healthy earth contains properties that help bolster our physical health. And, as mentioned above, being outdoors provides an extra boost of wellbeing and protects us from a number of mental and physical health ills. A bunch of different studies focused on daily gardening found that it reduced stress and BMI, at the same time as improving general health and life satisfaction.

If you don't have a garden, you can grow things on your window ledge or balcony. Or you can work in your local community garden or even try some surprising guerrilla gardening and fling seeds about!

Sing your heart out

Look, I am a *terrible* singer, but hear me out. Singing provides an instant boost to your system and it doesn't matter how awful that singing is.

Singing works muscles in the upper body and boosts the cardio-vascular system, encouraging more oxygen intake. It releases feel-good endorphins, increases alertness, improves immunity, reduces stress, improves brain function and promotes overall good health.

Singing in a group is the best way to reap the most health rewards, because the social connection we experience provides all kinds of 'feel well' benefits. But singing alone also switches on these brilliant responses that make us feel well. What am I suggesting, I hear you ask? I am suggesting that you turn on your favourite tune and sing along. You could belt it out in the car or in the kitchen – it really doesn't matter. Singing is a very easy, very fun way to take care of yourself … and you only need three minutes for most songs.

BEST SONGS FOR SINGING AT THE TOP OF YOUR LUNGS IN THE CAR OR KITCHEN (ACCORDING TO MY FRIENDS)

'I Try'
– Macy Gray

'We Are Family'
– Sister Sledge

'Chandelier'
– Sia

'Rehab'
– Amy Winehouse

'Sabotage'
– Beastie Boys

'Hotline Bling'
– Drake

'I Will Survive'
– Gloria Gaynor

'What's Up'
– 4 Non Blondes

'Wonderwall'
– Oasis

'Party in the USA'
– Miley Cyrus

'Old Town Road'
– Lil Nas X

'September'
– Earth, Wind & Fire

'You Oughta Know'
– Alanis Morissette

'Bohemian Rhapsody'
– Queen

'Wuthering Heights'
– Kate Bush

'Since U Been Gone'
– Kelly Clarkson

'Say My Name'
– Destiny's Child

'Let's Stick Together'
– Bryan Ferry

'Livin' on a Prayer'
– Bon Jovi

'I Can See Clearly Now'
– Jimmy Cliff

'I Believe in a Thing Called Love'
– The Darkness

'I Wanna Dance with Somebody'
– Whitney Houston

'Ain't No Mountain High Enough'
– Marvin Gaye & Tammi Terrell

'Man! I Feel Like a Woman'
– Shania Twain

'Islands in the Stream'
– Dolly Parton and Kenny Rogers

'Shallow'
– Lady Gaga and Bradley Cooper

Dance like nobody's watching

All that stuff we said about singing? A lot of it applies to dancing, too.

Recently, a University of Sydney study looked at the benefits of attending No Lights, No Lycra freestyle 'dancing in the dark' classes. The researchers found that 95 per cent of the participants agreed that the classes improved their physical health and 97 per cent also agreed that they improved their mental health.

You don't have to be a great dancer or go to a class (although classes add an extra social self-care win). Simply committing to one full track's worth of dancing around your kitchen or living room has excellent health benefits.

Move your body

Exercise has all kinds of mental health benefits, as well as the physical benefits we all know about. For instance, exercising regularly – even just taking a walk – helps to shape our 'fight or flight' response, making it less reactive. This is especially helpful if you suffer from anxiety (like me!).

Movement also shakes up the brain's reward centres, making us more receptive to the feel-good chemical, dopamine, as well as circulating it more generously. This helps us to feel more motivated, happier and more hopeful, and can ease some of the symptoms of depression.

New research has found that lactate – the substance that's created in our bodies when we exercise – may also provide protection against depression and anxiety.

Despite all that great news, when women have babies, they very often stop exercising. In a UK survey of 1000 mothers, six out of ten women said they felt like they were neglecting their families when they took the time to exercise. One trial that looked at how active non-parents, first-time parents and second-time parents were found that up to 50 per cent of adults reduced their physical activity once they had children.

This is a crying shame, because we know just how beneficial movement is for all humans. Lots of good things happen in our brains and bodies when we get moving, be it a stroll in the park or a run around the block. So push away any misplaced guilt you might be feeling, and get moving in your own way in the name of self-care, ASAP!

Perhaps you could start by tapping 'yoga with Adriene' into the YouTube search box. (Highly recommended, and lots of how-to videos ranging from very beginner to more advanced.)

Try sensory self-care

I love the idea of using our senses as a wellbeing toolkit. Sensory therapy is now widely used in occupational therapy. This makes so much sense, doesn't it? We've all got smells and tastes and sounds and textures and sights that make us feel happy and restored – smells associated with nature, for instance. Who doesn't love the smell of freshly blooming jasmine or a crushed eucalyptus leaf, a handful of rosemary or a forest after the rain?

Make a list of sensory stimuli that help you to feel joyful or relaxed, then put together your own sensory feel-good first-aid kit. You might include a fragrance you love, a special photo, an object you've collected that means a lot to you, something that feels lovely, a sweet treat and a ribbon in a colour you love.

You could compile a playlist that makes you feel good or have a go-to audio book for times when having someone read you a story will make you feel better.

LOVELY SMELLS

· Peppermint	· Orange	· Coffee
· Rosemary	· Strawberry	· Freshly baked bread
· Lavender	· Jasmine	· Crayons
· Eucalyptus	· Pine	· Your favourite flower
· Lemon	· Fresh-cut grass	· Your favourite perfume

Kindness as self-care

Perhaps you have heard of something called the 'helper's high'?
It's a reaction that happens when we do something nice for someone
else, as our clever brains release dopamine and serotonin into our
systems, strengthening our bonds to fellow humans and making
us feel good about ourselves.

This makes kindness an excellent form of self-care, one
that can take just a minute or two or be more involved,
depending on how you decide to serve up
your kindness.

SOME HELPFUL KINDNESSES TO TRY

Chat to a friendly stranger

•

Leave a care package on a friend's doorstep

•

Add some books to your local street library

•

Donate blood

•

Send a card to a friend or family member

•

Buy coffee for the person behind you

•

Help another parent out

•

Bake (or buy) a cake for a friend

•

Print some photos and send them to family

•

Let someone in line ahead of you

•

Let other cars merge in traffic

•

Volunteer in your community

•

Pick up litter in your local park

•

Donate to a food bank or favourite charity

•

Sponsor a child or animal

•

Teach someone a skill you know

•

Learn and practise the art of active listening

•

Pat a friendly dog

•

Start a walking group in your neighbourhood

•

Be free with your well-wishes

Creativity as self-care

Lots of creative pursuits count as self-care because practising them results in long-lasting wellbeing boosts.

Research has found that design-based activities such as painting, drawing, crafting, gardening and songwriting improved the wellbeing of those who practised them. A 2016 Otago University study also found that working on creative activities such as these could predict feelings of wellbeing the next day. In other words, the benefits of creative work are enduring and protective.

The changes we see as we work on these kinds of creative pursuits are bolstering, and the improvement we see in our skills is heartening, too. I call them 'progress practices' because they provide a tangible way of marking progress when things in our lives might be feeling a little bit 'groundhog day'.

Creative activities often have centuries of tradition and a whole community attached to them, so on top of all the learning and making and growing they promote, they also make us feel less isolated. And creativity promotes positive psychological functioning, which gives us a physical boost as well.

Of course, carving out time to spend creatively can seem pretty impossible when you have a busy family life, but it's absolutely worth it if you can.

While you might think spending time doing these things is frivolous or unimportant, that couldn't be further from the truth. You get a huge self-care tick from me for spending time on creative pursuits.

5 CREATIVE 'TO-DOS' FOR BEGINNERS

Take an online class via Skillshare or similar. You could try illustration, writing, painting, sewing, knitting, crochet, embroidery, weaving, woodwork ... the list goes on.

Write in a journal every day (or even every second day).

Think about what you loved to make as a child and revisit that.

Wander the aisles of your local art supply shop or craft store and wait for inspiration to strike.

Take a class via your local community centre or adult education centre.

Check in with yourself

Very often when we become parents, our own needs, wants, hopes and dreams get put on the backburner. This is super understandable, but also ... not necessary.

We've spoken a lot about all the different ways you can build looking after yourself into your day. But another important consideration is thinking about what you really want from life and whether you're heading in that direction. Granted, things can slow down to a snail's pace when you're caring for one or more kids, but even snails are on the move and you can be on the move – for your own benefit – too.

While all these ideas and strategies are at the top of your mind, why not take the time to consider what your goals are and how you can edge towards them? It can be tempting to think that you can tend to your own goals when your kids are more grown up, but the days are long and the years are short, lady. Now is the time to consider what you want, what you really, really want and start moving in that direction.

Put pen to paper and start documenting the things that you most want ... for you. Perhaps some of them will intertwine with things you want for your kids – things like living in the country or having a less demanding job or starting a new and more lucrative career – but they really don't have to. This is about figuring out what your dreams for yourself are and starting to move towards those dreams.

Your self-care strategy should include locking in time to work on these important goals, however strange and selfish that might feel. (Spoiler alert: it's not selfish!) Yes, your child's happiness is super important. But mums matter, too! So what do you really, really want for your life?

Do you want:

A job?

A different job?

To retrain?

To live somewhere else?

To spend more time on activities you love?

To start a special project?

To learn a new skill?

To study?

To speak to a careers counsellor?

To see a therapist?

To be a therapist?

Several of these things?

Something else?

70 SPEEDY SELF-CARE IDEAS FOR BUSY DAYS

1. Pat a pet (or someone else's pet).

2. Go outside and breathe deeply.

3. Sit on the back step and drink a cup of tea.

4. Sit on the front step and drink a glass of wine.

5. Write a postcard to a friend (and post it!).

6. Do some stretches via YouTube's 'Yoga with Adriene'.

7. Take a hot shower.

8. Light a nice smelly candle.

9. Make your bed nicely.

10. Warm up your PJs in the dryer and pop them on.

11. Listen to a Studio Ghibli soundtrack.

12. Get under the blankets for five minutes.

13. Call a friend or favourite family member.

14. Go op-shopping/thrift shopping.

15. Make pikelets (recipe on page 93).

16. Go flower spotting around your block.

17. Read a chapter of your favourite book.

18. Go to a nursery and buy some pansies.

19. Try a guided meditation.

20. Do some cloud spotting.

21. Ask for help.

22. Freshen up your bed linen.

23. Try a DIY hand massage.

24. Write in your journal.

25. Read a beautiful poem.

26. Talk to a therapist.

27. Tidy up your wardrobe.

28. Go to the gym.

29. Daydream.

30. Bake something good.

31. Volunteer to help someone.

32. Watch a rom-com.

33. Pop on a beauty mask.

34. Listen to a podcast.

35. Buy yourself a gift.

36. Go to the doctor.

37. Write a poem.

38. Go shopping for fruit and veggies.

39. Watch gentle videos on YouTube (try Liziqi).

40. Print out some favourite photos.

41. Take time away from screens.

42. Leave a kind note for a neighbour.

43. Write a story.

44. Pick a posy of borrowed blooms and foliage.

45. Take a very long walk.

46. Take a nap.

47. Take a bath.

48. Thank someone for something.

49. Brew some delicious coffee.

50. Whip up a smoothie.

51. Get your hands into the garden.

52. Listen for nature sounds.

53. Sing loudly in the car.

54. Have a little cry.

55. Take your medications.

56. Spend consciously.

57. Spend time with a favourite person.

58. Stock up on some nice tea.

59. Go for a run … or jog … or fast walk.

60. Head for the mountains.

61. Write a song.

62. Look at the stars.

63. Do some drawing.

64. Say a prayer.

65. Spend time by the beach or other watery place.

66. Plan a mini-break.

67. Go to a favourite cafe.

68. Hug someone you love.

69. Hug yourself.

70. Knit or sew or crochet something.

CHAPTER 6

JOIN
THE CLUB

*When you feel like
you've really messed up*

Help me, I've made a terrible mistake!

So you've made a parenting 'mistake' – smacking, squeezing, screaming, accidents, insults, health missteps, etc. Where to from here, you wonder, through some pretty terrible feelings and the tears of deep regret.

Mistakes are part of the fabric of parenting life, but you'd be forgiven for thinking they weren't. We may (unfortunately) slap our children in a fit of frustration or say things that are mean or hurtful. Babies get dropped. Toddlers run away. Preschoolers suddenly have holes in their teeth. Schoolkids are forgotten at pick-up time. You've called your teenager 'lazy', the word slipping from your mouth before you could stop it.

In these days of picture-perfect parenting and the contrastingly nasty rise of mum-shaming, mistakes are rarely talked about. The thing is, they happen ALL THE TIME. It's just that this push for perfection and rejection of how humans respond to the stresses of raising their young means mistakes are usually kept secret. They're rarely spoken of, unless they make the front page of your favourite news site, and the parents who make slip-ups or errors (i.e. all of us!) berate ourselves, struggle with guilt and feel horribly ashamed.

It's important to remember that when stuff-ups happen, we are in good company. Parents can't have it together all the time. Especially if they're overwhelmed, overscheduled and under-slept.

I spoke to some mums I know about their own parenting mistakes, asking them how they felt in the wake of their missteps. Perhaps, when you are navigating your next mum muck-up, you can find solace in the knowledge that others have gone before you and felt the things you are feeling. And that you will not always be juggling these feelings.

WHEN MUMS MAKE 'MISTAKES'

'Yelling. Shouting.
Anger. Frustration.
I was young
and emotionally
underdeveloped
when I had my babies.
I had no idea how
to manage these
emotions. I felt/feel
so sad, guilty and
confused. I loved/love
them so much.'
– **Michele**

'I felt guilt, shame,
a failure, not good
enough … every
negative feeling
in the book.'
– **Janina**

'Number one feeling:
guilt. I feel the enormity
of shaping young
people with my words
and actions. I know that
I remember vividly most
of the parenting slip-
ups my own parents
made and I really want
to limit them myself.
So I feel guilty when
I make one myself.'
– **Kylie**

'I felt completely
awful. Really sad
and disappointed in
myself. I cry a little
but then apologise
and keep on trying.'
– **Lily**

'In the hazy new baby
days, I looked at my
phone – for a stupid
work email – and she
fell off the bed. I'll
never forget it. I can
still hear the fall, and
the cry. Plus I still
check her head,
five years later.'
– **Jenny**

'I felt selfish,
impatient, guilty,
sad, ashamed.'
– **Rebecca**

'All I hear and see
is my mother when
this happens.'
– **Sue**

The feelings parents experience after making a parenting mistake can be horribly all-consuming. But let's remember that it's what you do in response to the 'mistake' that can make all the difference.

Accept and apologise

Accept wholeheartedly that you have made a mistake. Be open about it with yourself and your family, and especially with your child. Put your child first in this 'accept and apologise' response. It's important that they know you regret your actions and that their feelings are the priority here (not yours!).

Talk it out

Talking through what has happened with someone you trust can really help. It can provide perspective and remind you of who you were before this error and that you are strong and resilient enough to push through this hard adjustment.

Sometimes getting some extra help from a counsellor or psychologist can help you to work through the complicated feelings that some mistakes spark. Don't hesitate to do this. Chapter 10 has more information on accessing support.

In the case of parenting mistakes, shame is rampant. It's a good idea to remind yourself that deep-diving into that self-focused shame is not going to help you or your child. In fact, it's likely to stop you from responding to your child's needs compassionately and constructively.

Also, it's important to model a constructive and compassionate response to your child. Shame is not that.

Try 'I made a mistake' instead of 'I am a mistake' or 'I am my mistake'.

Brené Brown's definition of shame versus guilt – feelings that she describes as 'the emotions of self-consciousness' – is really useful to think about here:

Shame = I am bad. Guilt = I did something bad.

Tap out of shame

Separate yourself from your mistake. Yes, you made a mistake, but YOU are not your mistake. Your mistakes do not define your character, so try hard not to absorb the error you made as an intrinsic part of yourself.

Make amends

When things have calmed down, make amends for your mistake. This means speaking to your child honestly and sincerely, and letting your child know how you hope to avoid this ever happening again. Make a plan together so that your child can make their feelings known and feel reassured and safe.

Make
it a lesson

There are lessons to be found in hard times and our response to them tells us important things about ourselves. Think about how you reacted, what led up to this event and how you could respond more constructively if the situation was to crop up again.

Return
with kindness

Continue to be open about what happened when appropriate, again with your child's wellbeing front and centre of any chatter. Be kind, show remorse and give your child lots of demonstrative love. Reaffirm that you are sorry and that you're learning how to do better next time.

Maintain
perspective

This has happened. You can't undo it. But what you can do is use this challenge as an opportunity to understand yourself and your child better.

Guilt vs shame

As haunting as guilt after a parenting mistake can be, it's really not all bad. Guilt is a feeling associated with empathy. Empathy is positive and vital in the parent–child relationship … and in all relationships, in fact. Feeling guilt indicates that you're putting yourself in your child's position and trying to feel what you think they may be feeling.

When guilt pops up, you can note that you're connecting to your child, albeit in a challenging and quite shitty-feeling way. Guilt signals us to focus on our child and manage the impact of the mistake we made.

But with shame, it's different. When we focus on shame after we've had a parenting mess-up, it turns our attention inward, as we begin a horrible cycle of berating and being disappointed in ourselves.

In Brené Brown's book *Daring Greatly*, she explains that shame has the most power over us when we keep it a secret. She argues that being more open about this complex feeling and the circumstances that sparked it can help to take the sting out of its tail.

Note

If you feel like you're losing control regularly – if you are harming your children or putting them in danger – then it's important to get help from a doctor or mental health professional (see Chapter 10).

The lame shame game

It's all very well and good for me to tell you to tap out of shame, but it's not always as easy as that. Yes, we know that shame is directing our emotions back to ourselves in ways that don't help our child. But it's hard to stop feeling ashamed when something distressing has happened, you were (or felt) responsible and there were consequences to manage.

Shame is normal, but when we keep hooking into shameful feelings, it impacts us in a number of ways.

People who feel shame often are likely to have low self-esteem, but are also at risk of other mental health issues. Humans who exhibit this shame-proneness are likely to have symptoms of depression. There are also connections between having a propensity to shame and conditions such as generalised anxiety disorder and social anxiety disorder.

If shame is a bit of a go-to for you, it's vital to note these connections and consider how they're affecting your life and your family. Seeking support from a mental health professional via your doctor can help you unravel any related potential issues such as depression and anxiety – and help you to get a handle on that life-altering runaway shame.

Dear Pip

'I don't think I can forgive myself.'

Maybe your child has moved on from your error, but you are finding it hard to forgive yourself. Here are some ideas on feeling your way through these difficult times.

Create a personal mantra

Sometimes repeating some pragmatic and positive words can help prevent you from ruminating on what happened. Maya Angelou's 'now that I know better, I do better' is a great place to start, but you can write your own, too.

You could go for something like, 'Tomorrow's a fresh chance to have a better day' or 'I forgive myself and will keep trying' or 'I'm thankful for the chance to keep learning' or 'Good people sometimes make mistakes.'

Repeat your phrase five times if you find that you're having trouble shaking off those shameful feelings.

Take note

Write down your experience and all the feelings associated with it. Get every single thing down. Now turn to a fresh page and write down your strengths, the things you love doing, and the things you're most looking forward to.

Start a conversation with yourself

Name your harsh inner critic (in her book *Your Own Kind of Girl*, singer and author Clare Bowditch calls hers 'Frank') and when they pop up to tell you how terrible you are, chat to them about their scathing judgement.

INNER CRITIC:
'You screwed up.
You are a terrible
mother!'

YOU:
'Oh. Hi, Myron.
You're back.
That's a pretty mean
thing to say.
I'm a good mum, but
I'm also a normal
flawed human and
sometimes humans
bugger things up.'

MYRON:
'You totally
effed up!'

YOU:
'I did. But I'm sorry
about it, I'm making
amends, I'm trying
to do better.'

The more you practise these conversations, the easier it will be to ignore your inner critic.

Switch shame for steps

Take a leaf (see what I did there!) out of Chapter 5, get outside and get moving each day. Walking regularly gives you time to sort out your thoughts, exposes you to the health-boosting properties of the natural world and is an overall positive step in a fresh direction.

Try the 'best friend' approach

Treat yourself as you would your very best friend, should she find herself in your position. How would you speak to her? Care for her? Support her through this hard time? Afford yourself the same kind treatment and turn on your inner nurturer. Remember, you do not have to dole out your own personal penance for errors you make. You've been through enough.

Gather your own caring committee

In Rick Hanson's book *Resilient: How to Grow an Unshakable Core of Calm, Strength, and Happiness*, he suggests assembling a cast of supportive types (real or fictional) inside your head as a sort of army against negative self-talk. Rick's committee includes his close family, some favourite pals and fictional characters like *The Lord of the Rings*' Gandalf, *Star Trek*'s Spock and *Sleeping Beauty*'s fairy godmother.

Perhaps you don't have the kind of committee that Rick has? That's okay. Make up a committee of the size and strength that makes sense to you – fictional characters and the best sorts of people in your life included (whether they know it or not!).

Mine would include some close family and friends, my dogs, and a few current and former colleagues, plus author Marian Keyes, politician Alexandria Ocasio-Cortez, writer Caitlin Moran and actor Amy Poehler.

SOME CHARACTERS FOR YOUR CHEER
SQUAD COULD INCLUDE:

Jo March (from *Little Women*)

Polly Shelby (from *Peaky Blinders*)

Roxane Gay

Elizabeth Gilbert

Oprah Winfrey

Duckie (from *Pretty In Pink*)

Brene Brown

Lorelai Gilmore (from *Gilmore Girls*)

Jamie Fraser (from *Outlander*)

Helen Keller

(Thanks to my friends for these ideas!)

Of course, this caring committee commitment extends both ways when it comes to your real-life buddies and family members. Keep an eye out for them and check in with them often.

Breathe it out

Some deep breathing or a guided meditation when those unforgiving thoughts begin to swirl is really helpful. This eases shame's cousin, anxiety, and focuses you on the clever goodness of your body. It holds you up! It keeps you alive! It learns good things! It does good things! (Find more ideas on breathing exercises on pages 98, 166 and 180.)

Guess what? Children can be absolute nightmares sometimes. Their
actions and words can challenge even the calmest parent and make you
question if they care a jot about you (they almost always do!).

Many of the self-forgiveness strategies I've outlined are also really
useful when your child has pushed you to the edge of sanity. You can go
through them to centre and calm yourself when you actually would
rather throttle someone or run far, far away.

I also highly recommend sharing
these strategies with your child
(if developmentally appropriate)
so that they can tap into them
when they're feeling ticked off.
It can help greatly to have a joint
approach to managing those days
when things are not peachy.

Dear
Pip

'I'm not cut out to parent my kid!'

Are you the only one who has felt this way? No, dear reader, you are not. Every single parent who has drawn breath has navigated their own version of what you're struggling through.

Many parents find that when they have kids, their happiness dips rather than soars. Even if having a child was a life goal, the reality of managing oneself and another little person (or people) can be disappointingly challenging. And let's not even mention the often-challenging behaviour of bigger people!

'Healthy relationships definitely make people happier. But children adversely affect relationships,' wrote Jennifer Senior in 'All Joy and No Fun', a 2010 piece for *New York* magazine. She gives lots of examples, one in particular citing the work of psychologists Lauren Papp and E. Mark Cummings. They undertook a study of 100 long-married couples, asking them to document their disagreements for two weeks. Guess what? Nearly 40 per cent of the couples' arguments were about their kids.

So, you see, the very situation that made us want to make a baby – being in a happy, loving relationship – is then undermined by that child. Ugh. And clearly it's NOT just you feeling this way.

Parents' happiness is also affected by factors such as age, health, socioeconomic and marital status, and their support network. It's not surprising that these thoughts about being a crappy mum surface sooner or later. Many a mum is overworked, underpaid, underappreciated, exhausted and operating in survival mode. Some have children with disabilities or have disabilities themselves. They might have housing issues, money issues, relationship pressures ... the list goes on.

Some mums deduce that having difficulties and negative feelings about being a mother means that they're somehow failing.

I remember many, many occasions spent staring at the ceiling, eyes streaming, ears filling with tears, wondering what I had gotten myself into and how I was going to keep doing this for the next ten, fifteen, twenty, infinity years.

These feelings (and ear tears) are very often part and parcel of the parenting experience. The sooner we normalise them, the better. That said, normalising these feelings doesn't mean we should accept being pushed to the brink (at times). There are other ways of looking at these sad and hard moments.

We could note that these feelings are a clear sign that we need more support.

We could accept that these feelings are proof that we need to alter our course a little (if possible, and it isn't always possible) because the current approach is taking far too much of a toll.

These feelings are the red flags of mum life and a signal that, if all else fails, you need to slow every single thing right down, erase some things from your to-do list, say no to some stuff and recharge your batteries. The 'not cut out for this' mum feelings often mean that we need to cut out some stuff ... and catch a break – the sort of break that addresses the various difficulties that are making being a mum even harder.

You're not alone

I've collected some thoughts from *other* great mums who have felt they were not cut out for parenting at one time or another. Pop a sticky note in this page so you can quickly access their excellent advice.

'Just try to relax, know that you are doing your best and kids are remarkably resilient. But if you are concerned you will harm them then get help to deal with that.' – **Marg**

'You only see yourself from the inside, not how your children see you from the outside. While you think everything is going to pot your children are loving you to pieces. I think I need to tell this to myself more often … we underestimate how big their love is.' – **Shevonne**

'Having had three boys under five and one being autistic and having an intellectual disability, I quickly learned that it didn't matter if I made "mistakes" as these were "mistakes" in the eyes of those who were not walking in my shoes. You're allowed to be both a masterpiece and a work in progress.' – **Vicki**

'It's okay to not love your kids every day and every moment. That doesn't make you a bad mum! We don't expect that of any of our other relationships, so it's unrealistic to expect it of parenting. Go easy on your expectations of yourself (and your kids).' – **Natalie** (my cousin!)

'None of this parenting journey comes with a rule book or instruction manual. None of us really knew what we were signing up for but we are here and "good enough" parenting is absolutely fine. We may not take naturally to this responsibility but it is a responsibility we take seriously.' **– Defah**

'We're all learning on the job, and as long as the child has love, shelter and food, you're doing a great job.' **– Lexi**

'Best thing my shrink ever said to me is that the fact that you are worrying about being a crap mum automatically makes you not a crap mum, because if you really were doing a terrible job, you wouldn't care.' **– Fern**

'You're doing great, you keep getting up and getting on with it, and that's enough. At the end of the day, you are growing humans from children to adults, it's hard going and a mammoth job, when you stop to think about it. So go easy on yourself, little by little, don't try and do it all, invite others in to be mentors and friends to your children, if you can ... it takes a village, find yours – it's the biggest gift you could give yourself and your children.' **– Shelley**

Remember, it's not all down to you

The brilliant author Anne Lamott has plenty of wise advice for mothers. She notes that even parents who seem perfectly cut out for the job are often winging it. She also points out that our children are not the sum total of our efforts – and our rough days. There are lots of influences shaping them. (They even turned up pre-shaped with DNA and whatnot that predisposes them to certain ways of being.)

In a 2011 interview with website *Salon*, Anne says that parenting has meant coming to terms with the fact that we are not in control of how our kids turn out. She points out that wonderful parents can raise very challenging children, and parents who do very little can raise brilliant humans. As much as we'd like to believe it's all up to us … it's not!

That's not to say that we don't have a hope of influencing our child with our parenting, rather that a mismatch between the parent we thought we might be and the parent we actually are is something pretty much all of us experience. Our child is not a lump of playdough, ready to be shaped by their parents. So many other influences and experiences come into play.

Of course, parenting does impact children as they develop, but being a 'good enough' parent is what matters. And defining that for yourself (with some handy-dandy professional guidelines as discussed on pages 78–81) is key.

If you're measuring yourself against others' very involved and hands-on parenting, it's good to note that 'over-parenting' can have a detrimental effect on kids.

What qualifies as over-parenting, you might be wondering? It not only includes the accommodation we spoke about in Chapter 3, but also throws parental expectation and the pressure to perform — both academically and personally — into the mix.

This over-parenting may rob kids of important formative experiences and stop them acquiring skills they need to be happy, healthy humans.

In a 2020 piece for website *The Conversation*, University of Winchester lecturer in psychology Ana Aznar explained that children of all ages are affected by this sort of over-parenting. Ana says that it can contribute to shyness, anxiety and problems with kids' friendships.

So if you're not the perfect mum making mouse-shaped sushi for lunchboxes, shielding them from hard experiences, attending every school event, hanging off your child's every word and framing each piece of artwork, science say that's actually okay. In fact, it's probably very sensible.

And honestly? I tried to be that mum for a little while and there were no medals and I got very, very tired, very, very quickly.

Celebrating your parenting wins

Where do we begin when it comes to framing our own parenting with a more self-compassionate lens?

Let's go back to Anne Lamott for a wee bit more inspiration. Anne is now a grandparent and she says that she is working at remembering all the things she did beautifully when raising her son. Calling it a 'radical act', she talks of the hours she spent playing with Sam, reading him stories, sorting through Lego and bringing wonderful people into his life.

There's something special in this approach and I think we don't need to wait until we're grandparents to start tallying the things we do well as mums.

Next time you think you are 'not cut out for this', take a few steps back and think about marvellous mum moves. I am super-sure you have a bunch of them and you don't have to wait until your child is grown up with their own kids to appreciate them. Here are some places to start.

MARVELLOUS MUM MOVES

Picking up a kid in the middle of the night from a friend's house
•
Helping to blow child noses without being too rough
•
Listening even when you are really busy/tired
•
Identifying and understanding your child's friendship group
•
Watching a lot of kids' TV without complaining
•
Helping your child understand and manage feelings
•
Pulling together last-minute costumes
•
Putting your own feelings aside when your child reveals surprising truths
•
Making the exact right comfort food to suit the family mood
•
Detangling knotty hair very gently
•
Inventing alternative swear words
•
Looking after sick children/teenagers
•
Surrounding your child with wonderful adults to lean on
•
Taking small people's concerns seriously
•
Removing splinters expertly
•
Talking about bodies
•
Planning birthday parties
•
Supporting sporting endeavours, from training to trophies and tears
•
Encouraging a sense of community and social justice

PS: Clearly heaps of dads are good at these things, too!

CHAPTER 7

YOU'RE A GREAT MUM

When your best doesn't feel like it's enough

Zero to hero

You shifted into a whole new way of human-ing when you became a mum. Sometimes in survival mode, often putting yourself last, regularly shuffling your want-to-dos aside for the must-dos family life throws up, perhaps getting your heart broken some of the time, almost always becoming the 'default' person at your place ... the one who does all the things. (See Chapter 8 for more on that.)

Holy heck. It's an awful lot and you're doing it all with NO INSTRUCTION MANUAL!

With all that noted, it's vital to talk about how absolutely terrific you are. Not only were you able to birth a human (sometimes more than one), but you are kind of managing to grow and look after it, while you grow and look after yourself. I say 'kind of' because chances are some things *are* slipping through the cracks. If you are the sort of mum I am, you haven't got it all together and your days routinely seesaw between what you need to do and what your child needs from you.

If there was a Cirque du Soleil of mum life, I would be the one attempting to look snazzy in a leotard as I drop several sparkly balls and try not to think about my wedgie. Perhaps this is you, too. I'm guessing that you, like me, are constantly keeping your eye on all the urgent things in front of you and forgetting about all the brilliant things you have achieved prior to this moment.

You are doing this parenting thing with pretty much zero hands-on training. As you learn on your feet, the ground shifts under you, and you are often doing it with an audience, and someone small (or large) is quite frequently yelling at you. You, my friend, are a blinking HERO.

Another hero, a political journalist by the name of Gaby Hinsliff, sparked a conversation about the experience of motherhood when she wrote a piece for the *Observer* a few years ago, '"I had it all, but I didn't have a life"'. Gaby wrote about her work/kid balance struggle – a struggle she was fortunate enough to be able to step away from (she gave up working when her son was small). She described the contrasts of parenting with its paradoxes and irrationality.

Some people scoffed and said she should shut up, get on with it and stop complaining. (Those people were clearly idiots.) But one reader responded compellingly, noting that Gaby, herself, you, me, every mum you know had not been prepared for this big shift – that we are all scrambling to keep up and that it doesn't really ever end (but that's okay, I promise).

'From the seventies to the present day, girls and young women have been kept increasingly in the dark about this Great Irrationality,' commented this reader. 'No one hints to them that the moment the first child arrives the entire center of gravity of the mother's life changes forever. A mother can no longer see the world in the same way as she did because the lens of the child, even an adult child, is always there.'

NO-ONE tells you. Not really, truly in a way that we can understand anyway. As John Lennon sang, 'Nobody told me there'd be days like these.' Perhaps it's not even possible to tell us. Perhaps it's all just too big.

This is why it's important to give yourself props for all that you do in your efforts to adapt to this huge life change. This is why it's vital to notice the good bits and the progress you have made.

Stop the juggly forward momentum occasionally. Turn and look over your shoulder as you work hard to adjust to the trickery that is constantly coming your way. Do this even if you occasionally drop the ball. Actually, especially if you drop the ball. And keep doing it right through your parenting years (i.e. for the rest of your life!).

When you look back and focus carefully, you will see that you are doing a pretty bloody brilliant job of something that you have had very little schooling in. So know that.

There are lots of more formal ways of taking stock of your best mum – and woman – moments, past and present. A snazzy leotard is not even required for many of the following exercises (but you can wear one if you like!). Choose your favourite or try them all.

Mum moments/Me moments

Start collecting 'Mum moments' and 'Me moments'. Make note of the gains you are making by keeping a diary to track personal and parenting progress, even if you jot down just a few messily scribbled words. For example:

Mum moment

Said YES to my child when so very often I say NO without thinking.

Me moment

Sat in the sun at lunchtime and felt so much better for it.

Journalling can help you focus on and process thoughts and feelings, spot behavioural patterns, solve problems and set goals. This sort of Mum/Me journalling can also help you to appreciate when you are achieving and even surpassing those goals, because often we're on to the next challenge without congratulating ourselves on getting through the last one.

Flip back through the pages regularly to notice how much you're actually doing well and to refocus yourself on the moments that matter to you.

According to the experts, journalling has a whole bunch of physical and mental health benefits if you use it to help organise and process your thoughts.

'Scientific studies have shown it to be essentially a panacea for modern life,' Hayley Phelan wrote in her 2018 article, 'What's All This About Journaling?' in *The New York Times*. 'There are the obvious benefits, like a boost in mindfulness, memory and communication skills. But studies have also found that writing in a journal can lead to better sleep, a stronger immune system, more self-confidence and a higher I.Q.'

Reflecting on life as both a woman and a mum, even via a few short phrases each day, is a super-simple way to love yourself a little bit more. In fact, journalling these positive experiences can prompt your brain to 'relive' them and give you a helpful second dose of feel-good hormones.

If you find yourself loving the whole journalling thing (perhaps you are already an avid journaller), you could try a longer form of this excellent habit – author Julia Cameron's 'Morning Pages'. Julia, author of *The Artist's Way*, recommends busting out 'three pages of longhand, stream of consciousness writing' when you first wake up. She stresses that these pages are not supposed to be art, or even *writing*.

Morning Pages are an excellent way of getting whatever is swirling around in your head onto the page in one giant daily brain dump, freeing you up to think about other things and giving you some perspective on thoughts that might have been playing on your mind/torturing you. I highly recommend trying this, if you have time for it … even one page is worth doing, if that is all you can manage. You will feel better, stronger and less crappy for it!

Three good things

Sometimes called the 'What went well' exercise, this simple but genius habit can help you to notice the good job you are doing, even when your days seem to be a total shambles. Basically, you write down three good things you experienced each day, on a daily basis. For example:

Kiddo ate TWO-THIRDS of their dinner.

Read a chapter of my new book on the bus.

Snuck out to the shops by myself.

Clearly yours will be different to the list above. Or not. They are all good things.

This activity cleverly worms its way into your thought processes and, before you know it, you're operating from a much more positive and curious default. You begin to realise what matters to you most, and gravitate towards making more time for those things.

When you're a parent, it can be extremely helpful to include the everyday meaningful moments you experienced with your child, however fleeting or tiny they might have been. Before you know it, you have a whole list of mum achievements and ace times you've spent together – quite the handy bucket list if you're stuck for something special to do together.

The benefits of this activity are long lasting. A 2005 study by psychologist Martin Seligman and colleagues, published in *American Psychologist*, found that writing about three good things was associated with an increase in happiness immediately after documenting the three things, as well as one week, one month, three months and six months later.

Dear Pip

'I'm NOT a great mum (sigh).'

Life can deal us a bunch of circumstances that can lead to us feeling like we are just a bit … shit. If you feel like this, I am sorry that you're going through it. I have been there and sometimes I still feel this way. It's a very weighty and difficult feeling to contend with.

Thankfully, there are lots of strategies that can help mums who feel this way feel much better. Speaking to someone about it can be a total life-changer (turn to Chapter 10 for more on that).

For now, let's talk about ways you can start to address any negative feelings you have about your (excellent) self. It's important to resist thinking the worst of yourself, if you possibly can, because those sorts of thoughts can trigger anxiety and depression (or be symptoms of anxiety and depression – hence talking to a professional is a great idea!).

I have dragged around various self-esteem situations for most of my life. From high to low to rock-bottom, I've felt it all. I suspect that I am not the only one to feel this way, to feel that I'm not enough, not keeping it together, that I'm a hideous sort of person. Perhaps you have felt one or more of these feelings, too? Chances are you have, because you are here reading this, girlfriend!

So, what are we aiming for? What *is* healthy self-esteem? Folk who have healthy self-esteem routinely like themselves and they value their achievements. It's their default.

You. Are. An. Excellent. Person.

Unfortunately, mums are prone to not like themselves and may gloss over their successes. Mums can be incredibly self-critical, forgetting to keep an eye out for their wins and instead flagging every time they feel they've tripped up with a rock-solid episode of hating on themselves. It. Is. Terrible.

If you behave this way, constantly putting yourself down and facing every knocked-over hurdle with an intrusive barrage of thoughts about how much you suck ... you're on a slippery slope to other isolating and distressing behaviours.

Why do we feel this way? There are a bunch of different reasons. Perhaps one or more of these might feel a tiny bit like you:

Negative experiences contribute to you telling negative stories about yourself.

Someone significant has (or had) too-high expectations of you.

Your expectations of yourself are too high, so you set yourself up to fail.

You haven't stopped to consider all your excellent qualities and skills.

You're caught in a pattern of difficult times that's reinforcing negative feelings about yourself.

Low self-esteem can chip away at your quality of life and, before you know it, you might find yourself exhibiting one or more of the following behaviours:

Feelings of shame, guilt, anger, anxiety, sadness and/or depression due to habitual self-criticism

•

Relationship problems due to feeling inadequate or under pressure or deserving of suffering

•

Self-isolating because of the fear that others will judge you as harshly as you judge yourself

•

Overcompensating and/or focusing on perfectionism in an effort to make up for perceived failings

•

Ignoring or neglecting opportunities and responsibilities

•

Becoming passive in your exchanges with other people

•

Neglecting self-care

•

Exhibiting self-destructive behaviours (such as drinking too much, disordered eating or drug use) – also side effects of battling constantly with feelings about ourselves

•

Suffering physical and/or mental ill health in general

Ugh. This stuff can be really debilitating, can't it? Luckily, you can stop being mean to yourself and start LOVING your bits – both brilliant and bumpy – right now, with a fortifying dose of self-compassion.

What is self-compassion?

Self-compassion is ... being compassionate to yourself. *Quelle surprise!*
It means that you like yourself whether things are going great or are pretty
pear-shaped. Being self-compassionate means that you understand that
you are good and lovable, no matter what is happening in your life. And it
means forgiving yourself when you mess up and being kind to yourself
by default.

As psychotherapist Tim Desmond, author of *The Self-Compassion Skills
Workbook*, says: 'Self-compassion allows us to take good care of ourselves
when we are faced with life's inevitable difficulties.'

It's not something that needs to be earned. Soak that up.

Many of us are not just caring for kids, but for others, too. To look at
the way we try so blinking hard and run ourselves ragged, you'd think that
perhaps there is some sort of points system for compassion, that without
pushing ourselves we don't deserve to be treated beautifully. Thankfully,
that is simply not so. Humans deserve compassion from the get-go.
And you deserve self-compassion, no matter what.

So how do you rustle up some compassion for your good self when
you are mostly used to telling yourself off and feeling like you're falling
short? Let's talk about that.

Identify your favourite bits of you

Start thinking about those positive qualities you keep tucking away and –
for the most part – ignoring.

Make a list of those right now. You don't have to show this list to anyone,
but in your more bracing self-berating moments, you can pull it out and set
the record straight and remember that it's 'kindness first' when it comes to
dealing with yourself. Here are some ideas to get you started.

YOUR FAVOURITE BITS OF YOU

fun

curious

diplomatic

sensitive

determined

persistent

pragmatic

considerate

generous

optimistic

cheerful

hardworking

loving

trustworthy

resilient

intuitive

adventurous

creative

loyal

ambitious

kind

intelligent

passionate

compassionate

entertaining

friendly

diligent

energetic

honest

understanding

insightful

calm

observant

patient

disciplined

collaborative

sincere

caring

brave

funny

practical

forgiving

helpful

easy-going

witty

vulnerable

organised

tolerant

dependable

reliable

Treat yourself nicely – self-compassion 101

Self-compassion activates the part of our brain scientists refer to as the 'care circuit', emitting helpful hormones and making us feel good.

Years ago I spoke to a friend about things that make me feel okay when life is tough, and one of those things was putting my hand over my heart and breathing deeply. 'I don't know why it settles me down, but it really does,' I told her.

It turns out that I was intuitively on the right track. One of self-compassion's most revered researchers, Kristin Neff, suggests that touch is the key here. 'One easy way to care for and comfort yourself when you're feeling badly is to give yourself supportive touch,' she explains. 'Touch activates the care system and the parasympathetic nervous system to help us calm down and feel safe.'

So that hand-over-heart touch may help to activate that care circuit, turning on the experience of warmth, caring and compassion.

If you feel a bit weird about the hand-over-heart move, there are other ways that you can promote self-compassion and its associated benefits, through self-soothing touch. (Yep, it's not just for babies!)

SELF-SOOTHING MOVES

Cup your hands together in your lap.

Cross your arms and give yourself a secret hug.

Stroke your arm.

Put one hand on your abdomen.

Place one hand on your cheek.

Hold your face in your hands.

Practising self-compassion also seems to help strengthen the parts of the brain that make you happier, more resilient and more attuned to others, according to psychotherapist Tim Desmond.

Three-step self-compassion

If you're feeling out of sorts (not good enough, disappointed, stressed, sad, worried, ashamed or any number of other difficult emotions), here is something to try.

1. **Hand on heart.** Stop, place your hand over your heart and notice what you are thinking and feeling in your mind and your body. Try to name each feeling and sensation as you breathe deeply.

2. **Accept.** Speak kindly to yourself about what you are going through. 'You're doing it tough right now. You're suffering. It's okay to feel this way. Others have felt this way, too. This is tough.' Breathe and sit quietly as you deal with the hard stuff.

3. **Support.** Tell yourself that you are feeling what you need to feel, and that you can find a way through this. There are good reasons for difficult emotions. 'You are strong. Be patient with yourself.' Have faith in yourself to manage and process your situation in your own way.

Helpful behaviours
when you're feeling low

If things are on a bit of a downhill spiral when it comes to being nice to yourself, here are some ways to reset and some things to look out for.

Check in with yourself. What do you need to feel okay?
How can you show yourself the same kindness you'd show others?

Make time to do the things you love and be open to new opportunities.

Try to be open-minded when things get tough.
Humans are remarkably resilient and we can find our way through situations that seem impenetrable. Trust yourself to do that.

Watch out for avoidance, escape or safety-seeking behaviours that keep you trapped in this cycle. If things are going this way, refresh your self-compassion practice, or seek support from a trusted buddy, family member or healthcare professional.

Similarly, keep an eye out for self-neglect, social withdrawal and self-imposed isolation. Again, brush up on your self-compassion and/or seek support if you are starting to feel this way. And know that you are NOT alone. Lots of brilliant people have felt terrible about themselves, endured this sort of rough trot and come out the other side. You are in good company, treading your path alongside a legion of other great, loving, mistake-making, big-hearted mums.

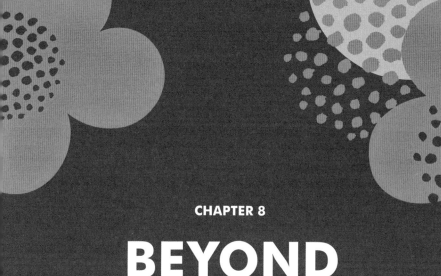

CHAPTER 8

BEYOND
TIRED

*When you feel like
you're doing all the work*

Being the default person

If you feel like you're doing it all and it's not really being appreciated ... If you feel like you are the default person for ALL THE THINGS at your house ... If you are feeling bloody exhausted much of the time ... Guess what? There are a bunch of other mums out there feeling a lot like you are. And I think, if they could, they would extend their arms and give you a giant cuddle because this is such a hard position to be in.

Let's talk a little bit about just how understandable it is that you feel this way. Let's also talk about how URGENT it is for society on the whole and also the people in our world who care about us to help address this huge issue.

A friend told me about the time she sat in a counselling session with her partner when her kids were fairly young. The counsellor asked them both to describe their typical days and they recounted them, her with resignation (early rising with the kids, domestic stuff, kid stuff, work stuff, domestic stuff, kids stuff, dinner, domestic stuff, bath, early to bed), him cavalierly (later rising, cafe breakfast, work, lunch at pub, work, home, domestic stuff, telly, late to bed).

When the counsellor asked why my friend was getting up with the kids at six (or earlier) each day while her partner stayed snuggled up until eight, he confidently replied that she was a morning person and enjoyed it. It was her kind of thing, he confided. Except it wasn't.

The situation was very similar at my house when I had young kids. I was exhausted and worried and depressed. I got up at six (sometimes five) to read Harry Potter books or watch cartoons on the couch because my sons needed a parent to supervise, feed and cuddle them.

I do not regret a single moment of those mornings (okay, I do wish I'd had a few more sleep-ins, I admit), but I get an empty feeling in the pit of my stomach when I think about how convenient it is for one partner to default to the other with that sort of 'her thing' excuse.

War and wisdom and craft, oh my!

The work ethic and responsibilities of women have been mythologised to the point of breaking them.

These mythological women – let's call them 'Athenas', after the Greek goddess of wisdom, war and craft (how appropriate!) – are on standby to fulfil the needs of their families around the clock. They care for the children and work both in and out of the home, often juggling more than one of these responsibilities simultaneously and also fulfilling other caring roles as best as they can.

These Athenas are in constant motion, planning for tomorrow, next month and next year while giving their all to today. They are struggling under the physical and mental load as they attempt to be 'good women' and 'good daughters' and 'good mothers'.

The load is so hefty that many put aside the things they most want to do, and their own wellbeing. They may even reduce their working hours in an attempt to accommodate the never-ending to-dos. They want to be available to their families to ensure the very best outcomes as they raise their kids … but they fail to be there for themselves.

The sacrifices these Athenas make result in a slowed career path and impact on their future financial health through reduced superannuation and savings, but it's a price they pay to keep some 'balance' in their life.

You deserve better. You truly do.

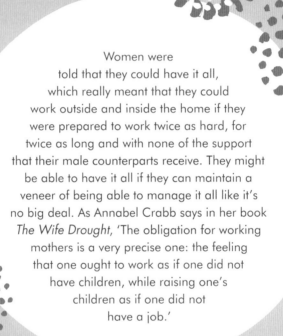

Women were
told that they could have it all,
which really meant that they could
work outside and inside the home if they
were prepared to work twice as hard, for
twice as long and with none of the support
that their male counterparts receive. They might
be able to have it all if they can maintain a
veneer of being able to manage it all like it's
no big deal. As Annabel Crabb says in her book
The Wife Drought, 'The obligation for working
mothers is a very precise one: the feeling
that one ought to work as if one did not
have children, while raising one's
children as if one did not
have a job.'

Truth. Gosh, it's no wonder we're feeling tired and freaking peed off. It's a justifiable way to feel whether you are working in the home or outside of it. This impossible balance has disadvantaged women from day dot.

How did we end up here?

Back in 1989, sociologist Arlie Hochschild wrote a book called *The Second Shift*. She researched and documented the domestic disparity at home, noting that most women follow their work day with a 'second shift' at home.

Arlie found that women were reliably doing the lion's share of caring for children and domestic duties, and discovered that women worked an extra month of 24-hour days each year compared with their husbands. 'These women talked about sleep the way a hungry person talks about food,' she explained, and you're probably nodding your head in solidarity.

The pressure on mums is really, really tough – tough enough to make you feel TIRED all of the time and UNAPPRECIATED very, very often.

A 2015 Australian study found that women are more likely than men to rush, and even when they are employed, they do more caregiving. 'Women may face more time commitments in total,' the study reported, 'and proportionally more of their time will be unrewarded by income: all could contribute to gender differences in health.'

Gender differences in health? Think about that for a moment. And think about your health. Now keep reading.

The 2016 Australian Census found that the average woman spends between five and fourteen hours a week doing unpaid domestic duties. The average man? He clocks up less than five hours a week. Good on you, mate.

Of course, some men are doing more than five hours a week. I know that. But on average the gents are stopping at five. Think about that for a moment. And think about your health again. Now keep reading because there's more you need to know.

'You should've asked!'

Fast-forward a titch to 2017 (almost 30 years after *The Second Shift* was published) and French artist and computer science engineer Emma addressed this unsustainable workload in a comic that speedily (and quite rightly) went viral.

Perhaps you saw it? It was called *The Mental Load* and it featured a mum trying to juggle all the usual things – tidying up, cooking dinner, feeding children, thinking about work, entertaining guests, pouring drinks … eventually it all collapses around her and her husband cries that she should have asked him for help. The comic then goes on to show exactly what's happening behind the scenes in this overburdened mother's mind.

'When a man expects his partner to ask him to do things, he's viewing her as the manager of household chores,' Emma explained in the comic, noting that this positions the man as her underling. 'The problem with that, is that planning and organising things is already a full-time job.'

Emma says that asking women to do the organising as well as participate in the doing means that they end up doing three-quarters of all the domestic work. But you probably already know this.

There is little wonder that mums are feeling time pressed, stressed and possibly even depressed, as Leah Ruppanner, Senior Lecturer in Sociology at The University of Melbourne, puts it. 'The challenge is not housework alone but the way in which housework is embedded within broader care responsibilities,' Leah said in a 2017 piece she wrote for

The Conversation. She also referred to Sarah Fenstermaker's *The Gender Factory: The Apportionment of Work in American Households*, which features the sad hypothesis that 'husbands may require more household work than they contribute'.

By 2018, the Australian Human Rights Commission was telling us even more about the time women spend looking after others and how they're rewarded for their work.

Ninety-five per cent of primary parental leave (outside of the public sector) is taken by women, and women spend almost three times as much time taking care of children each day, compared to men.

Australian women account for 68 per cent of primary carers for older people and people with disabilities.

While women comprise roughly 47 per cent of all employees in Australia, they take home on average $251.20 less than men each week. The national gender 'pay gap' is 15.3 per cent and it has remained stuck between 15 per cent and 19 per cent for the past *two decades*.

The cost of it all

At the tail end of a visit to my doctor (where I had gone to speak about my own exhaustion), I chatted about this domestic dilemma and how it might be undermining women's health. I figured there must be a whole other layer of health-related disparity at play – one that we're not talking about enough.

Dr Jeannie confirmed that, especially during the COVID-19 pandemic, it was one of the top things her patients were discussing with her. While in the 2020 lockdown, women had the time to think more about the load they were carrying and they were pretty cross about the whole darn thing. Rightly so. This difference in the mental and domestic load means that women have less time to do the things that make them feel happy, they may be seething with resentment or disappointment for/in their partner and, to top it all off, the stress they are living with every day is damaging their mental, physical and financial health.

Financial health is hugely problematic, in fact. According to Verve Super's 'Make Our Future Fair' campaign, Australian women are retiring with 47 per cent less super than men – time off to have children is a major contributor to this statistic – and one-third of single older women live in poverty.

All of this is not okay. And if any of this sounds like you … OF COURSE you have a right to be upset about it. Maybe it's time to explore strategies to protect yourself from these harms.

Time intensity and time poverty

A seventeen-year study by The University of Newcastle (Australia) and the University of Hohenheim (Germany) confirmed that time pressure was taking a huge toll on women. Factors such as the number of children they had, their work security, financial pressures and the hours they needed to work turn the screws more tightly on stress.

The study authors noted that childcare and parental leave reforms could provide women with some relief and aid more balance at home, but clearly there's more to the story than that. Women are generally the ones who are dealing with frequent or time-sensitive domestic tasks and this grind is wearing them down in a whole bunch of ways.

THE 'NO WONDER YOU'RE TIRED' LIST

If you're still not convinced that your fatigue is justifiable, take a look at these unpaid duties that many of us participate in. How many of the things on this list are you doing?

Travelling to and from a place of paid employment

•

Household errands, such as shopping, banking, paying bills and keeping financial records

•

Housework, such as preparing meals, washing dishes, cleaning the house, washing clothes, ironing and sewing

•

Outdoor tasks, including home maintenance (repairs, improvements, painting, etc.), care maintenance or repairs and gardening

•

Volunteer or charity work (for example, canteen work at the local school, unpaid work for a community club or organisation)

•

Playing with your children, helping with personal care, teaching, coaching or actively supervising them, or getting them to child care, school or other activities

•

Looking after other people's children (aged under twelve years) on a regular unpaid basis

•

Caring for a disabled spouse or disabled adult relative, or caring for elderly parents or parents-in-law

This list comes from the Household, Income and Labour Dynamics in Australia (HILDA) Survey. Don't you feel tired just reading it?

Effects of stress on the female body

Stress is affecting your body in a bunch of ways, with sleep disruption at the tiptop of the list and contributing to that ever-present tiredness. But there are lots of other ways that rushing about, being on edge, worrying, being overloaded with to-dos, relationship tension and a whole laundry list of other mum and woman difficulties can take a toll on your health.

THESE HEALTH ISSUES MAY INCLUDE:

- Depression and anxiety
- Migraines
- Diabetes
- Headaches
- High blood pressure and elevated heart rate
- Body aches and pains
- Weight gain
- Digestive issues
- Menstrual issues
- Fertility issues
- Decreased sex drive

If you read that and thought, 'Shit. Yes. I really need to do something about this mess!', fear not. The time is ripe for change. Let's find some strategies to cope with some of that stress and then we'll look at how to share the load.

10 simple, energising, stress-banishing tips

Here's a little go-to list for when you're really struggling. These tips are not going to shift the workload at your place, but they can help you feel less overwhelmed, which will help you feel less tired.

1. **Deep breaths and mindful breathing** Breathing deeply and practising mindfulness (see page 97) can stop you from spiralling into panic or catastrophising, and help your body get the oxygen it needs. You could learn some deep-breathing techniques via an app and bust them out when you're feeling wrung-out.

2. **Write it down** Getting all the things that are on your mind down on paper can help you feel less exhausted and make the very, very tricky seem slightly more doable. Head to Chapter 2 for more on this.

3. **Simple stretches** Stretches, be they informal or of the yoga kind, can help to energise your body and get the blood flowing so you can feel your best.

4. **Walking** Walking might seem impossible when you're feeling tired, but it's a great way to restore perspective, get your body working optimally and reset your weary brain. Some days I walk to the corner and back, other days around the entire neighbourhood. Every little bit counts.

5. **Talk it out** Whether you talk to a friend or head to a professional, talking through what's going on can really help to not only shift a load off your shoulders, but also to work out some strategies to make things feel less frantic.

6. **Time out** Admittedly this is not always simple, but even ten minutes to yourself can sometimes be enough to reboot your brain and feel a tiny bit more restored.

7. **Take a shower or bath or swim** Water has all kinds of superpowers, and providing comfort to weary mums is one of the least talked about. Even the simple act of splashing cold water on your face can send blood to your vital organs, helping to reduce anxiety. Of course, a hot shower is much nicer, if you can manage it!

8. **Lie down and try a guided meditation** Snuggle under a blanket for five minutes, then breathe and feel your way through a calming or bolstering meditation (with some help from an app such as Smiling Mind).

9. **Head outside** I don't know about you, but the minute I step outside into somewhere with greenery, I begin to feel better about the world and all its beauty (even when I'm utterly exhausted).

10. **Sensory first aid** Turn to your sensory first-aid kit (see page 121) and liberally apply your favourite for an instant boost.

How to begin to share the load more fairly

If you are parenting with another person, let's look at some ways you can work together to share the work that parenting and family life bring.

Take note

Rather than write down all of the specific mum to-do things that shit you (although I'm all for a bit of journalling about that!), take note of the ways that society manipulates women into the do-almost-all role with outdated social support structures, societal pressure and sneaky Athena-promoting media messaging. Get a grasp of the bigger picture. Look around you next time you're watching TV or in the playground or at the supermarket. You will probably see other tired women struggling in the same ways as you. It could all be so different if women were better supported by our communities.

Unpack the mental load together

Show your partner this chapter. Talk to them about how much the 'worry work' on top of all the other work is weighing you down.

Sometimes clarifying that this carer/breadwinner stereotype is a societal issue as well as an issue at your place can make this discussion less fraught. It's *not* just you. It's happening everywhere and women have been roped into this domestic default as a result of decades of cajoling by those who favour more traditional roles.

THE UNSEEN WORK OF FAMILY LIFE

· Remembering and planning for birthdays
· Keeping track of school communication and activities
· Being educated on and adapting parenting approaches
· Healthy meal planning
· Managing work to fit in with family life
· Being mindful of your child's needs and stress points
· Monitoring physical and mental health
· Nurturing spiritual wellbeing
· Teaching 'how to be a good person' type things
· Researching schools
· Managing medical appointments
· Sorting out/delegating household chores
· Curating cultural experiences
· Being the primary contact for child care and school
· Taking care of budgeting, saving and investments
· Managing pets
· Managing the family's clothing needs
· Remembering clothing and shoe sizes
· Overseeing homework and assessments
· Planning and executing holidays
· Keeping an eye on house and garden maintenance
· Ensuring medication is on hand
· Paying for and maintaining the family car
· Sorting out after-school and weekend activities
· Optimising schedules for happiness
· Monitoring and managing household supplies
· Understanding kids' friendships
· Liaising with child-related government organisations
· Managing public transport requirements
· Ensuring kids have age-appropriate toys and technology
· Making plans for the future

Be on the same team

It's hard to enter these discussions without getting emotional, but if you're focused on the goal of making things fair for you both and more peaceful for the whole family, you can work towards that together.

Quantify the problem at hand

Together, take stock of every single domestic duty at your place. This really needs to be a joint effort – none of this 'one partner presenting the other with a completed spreadsheet of household to-dos' or one partner saying, 'whatever you think, you know best'. Go room by room and nut it out as a team. The bills on the kitchen table could spark discussion about who deals with budgeting. The suitcases under your bed might prompt a chat about how you manage holiday planning. The giant pile of laundry is a chance to even up the playing field there. Use the list on page 183 if you need ideas.

Next, work together to delegate the duties fairly between all members of your family. You might choose to delegate based on skill, preference, time taken, time available, frequency or urgency. Are there any tasks you can outsource to give you both more time to do other things?

Because we live in techy times, there are a bunch of apps that can help with this delegation. This can be a slightly less emotional way of distributing tasks and avoiding those understandable spats about who's doing more/much more/too much. They include S'MoresUp, Picniic and Cozi.

Aim to focus on the future and put a new plan in place that covers all the tasks, distributing them fairly. If you need to talk through how things *were* working and how mad and tired that was making you, I'd wholeheartedly recommend doing that with a counsellor to achieve the most constructive results.

Have a stand-up meeting every week

Treat your family's to-dos in the same way that a business would, delegating tasks and making contingency plans together. Be sure you both bring a notepad or diary to the meeting.

Don't sabotage each other's efforts

If your partner is completing tasks differently to you, it's vital that you don't step in to save them. If something is really bugging you, discuss it as calmly as you can in one of your stand-up meetings and ask if your partner has any thoughts to share on your duties. This can, of course, be a bit fraught, so it's another good one to speak to a counsellor about.

Get some professional help

There are all kinds of family situations where it's not easy to get this workload balance right.

Perhaps you are a stay-at-home mum and your partner says the home/child care is your responsibility while the breadwinning is his/hers.

•

Your partner may disagree with you on what 'needs' to be done (for example, organising a birthday party, managing playdates, cleaning out the vegetable drawer in the fridge), sparking frustration and conflict.

•

You might divide things up between you and then you still can't manage the workload or your partner doesn't follow through with the allotted tasks.

If things are complicated at your place, it's vital that you get some support. This might mean seeing a counsellor on your own to manage your feelings and strategise a way forward. Or perhaps you might be able to seek counselling together with the aim of nutting out the imbalance at your house. This has the extra benefit of creating a safety net where you can talk about any other issues that are worrying you at home or work.

If you are parenting alone

Lots of mums are raising their kids without a significant other. This might be because you have separated or divorced and your partner is no longer involved with your kids. Or because your child/children's other parent has passed away. Or because you have chosen to raise your kids without a partner.

This brings its own challenges, depending on your circumstances. You are not able to rely on a second income and you have only yourself to rely on when it comes to all those bloody domestic duties. You have no option but to carry the load, but there may be family members or friends that you can share it with.

I have been a solo parent twice in my life and I understand that the joy of not having to deal with a partner's needs/wants is offset by worrying about money, domestic fatigue, playtime fatigue and loneliness. Solo mums are carrying the MEGA-mental load, and managing it is a huge challenge.

A loving support network is always vital to you and your child, but even more so if you are in the solo parent situation. Turn to pages 16, 25 and 189 for more ideas on building that.

Dear
Pip

'I'm not great at asking for help.'

I am the Queen of Not Asking For Help. So please, do as I say, not as I do.

Now that my children are grown up, I can see that reaching out for help could have led me to forge stronger bonds with the people around me. It could also have helped me to manage the practical tasks of parenting, to feel more loved and appreciated, and to have built more of a friendly network for my children to tap into.

When you ask for help from those around you, you're setting up yourself and your child for a lifetime of support. Not only that, you're creating opportunities to help those around you in return. This is not only a lovely exchange, but everyone also gets to tap into the wellbeing-promoting 'helper's high', turning on feel-good hormones and making us feel better about ourselves and the world around us.

How to ask for help

What kinds of help might you need?
It's likely and normal that you will
need varying combinations of support.

You are not Athena and you don't
need to do this alone. Let other
people in, if you possibly can.

Emotional support
someone to talk through life
and parenting challenges

Social support
someone to care for your kiddo
so you can have some time out

Practical support
someone to help you get the
domestic (or other) stuff done

GETTING SOME HELP
Make a list of the sort of help that would be meaningful to you and your child.

Then slowly, step by step, start tackling each
'help wanted' item on your list. Some helpers could be:

Family members

•

Friends

•

Trusted people in your community
(perhaps neighbours or other nice parents from child care or school)

•

Trusted people from work or study

•

Counsellors

•

Your doctor

•

Telephone counselling services

•

Reputable online forums

If you *can't* let others in, it could be a brilliant idea to talk to a therapist about this. Both you and your child could really benefit from extending your family and friends network. Chat to your doctor about accessing this kind of valuable support.

Remember, there are no medals for toughing things out on your own. It's much better to assemble your own kind and compassionate team to experience life alongside.

CHAPTER 9

YOU AND
ME BOTH

*When other people
are getting you down*

Unsolicited advice, judgement and comparison

We live in strange times. We are exposed to more information than ever before and at the same time we're fielding a heady cocktail of comparison and criticism as we navigate our days.

For mums, this is especially true, with the three pesky prongs of unsolicited advice, judgement and comparison combining their crappy powers in ways that may have us feeling utterly terrible, at least some of the time.

If you look more closely at these snarky prongs, you'll realise that they have something in common and that is the ability to make women feel anxious and isolated. Hooray. (Not.)

Let's talk about that, because chances are you will recognise some of yourself or some people you know. And let's also talk about how to protect yourself against the wrath of these pesky prongs.

The cost of unsolicited advice: isolation and anxiety

In 2017, *The New York Times* reported on a survey of mothers that focused on criticism and judgement. University of Michigan researchers spoke to 475 mothers about whether they felt judged for their parenting skills. A fairly surprising 61 per cent of the mums said that they had been judged for their parenting. (I say surprising, because I would have thought the figure would be higher.)

The co-director of this research, Sarah Clark of the University of Michigan's Child Health Evaluation and Research Center, said that the bulk of the criticism came from those who should know better. 'What stood out was the perception among so many more mothers that criticism is coming from folks within their own family,' she wrote. But it's not just family members who make the list of critics.

WHO'S CRITIQUING MUMS?

A mum's own mother or father – 37 per cent

A spouse or the child's other parent – 36 per cent

The in-laws – 31 per cent

Peers or friends – 14 per cent

Other mums in public spaces – 12 per cent

A healthcare provider – 8 per cent

People on social media – 7 per cent

A childcare provider – 6 per cent

One in four of the mums surveyed had been criticised by three or more of the above groups ... and that comes as no surprise at all. The mums polled made it very clear that they were fed up to the eye teeth with people weighing in on the job they were working so hard at.

An understandable 62 per cent of mums in this survey agreed that mums get lots of unhelpful advice from others. And 56 per cent said that mums cop too much of the blame and not enough of the credit for their children's behaviour. Hear, hear!

You might be wondering what these mums were being critiqued for. In order, the top-of-the-pops topics commented on were:

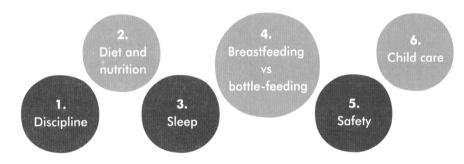

2. Diet and nutrition

4. Breastfeeding vs bottle-feeding

6. Child care

1. Discipline

3. Sleep

5. Safety

Sound familiar? Sigh. I thought so. It's enough to make any mum hunker down and steer clear of those critical people. Which is … exactly what many do. (Perhaps you are one of the many.)

'About half of the moms said they avoid certain people who give too much criticism,' Sarah Clark confirmed. That includes critical grandparents, aunties and friends.

So mums who are in need of the support of family and friends may step away from that network and become isolated, anxious and even depressed, all because the people closest to them underestimate just how undermining and upsetting their criticism – both overt and covert – can be. Some of those critics might think they are being helpful by 'troubleshooting' a mum's parenting. But the research tells us that this sort of troubleshooting is best coming from a mum's doctor or a trusted childcare professional.

Perhaps you have found yourself in this situation. It can be bolstering to know that other mums have felt just like you, and however well-intentioned that criticism is, it can undermine and isolate the tired women who are just trying to do their best, for goodness sake.

If you have been on the receiving end of this sort of nonsense, please accept a virtual hug from me. I would not like to name names here, but know that I am in that club, too. I found that it left me spending a lot of time second-guessing my choices and ruminating on my actions, and it diminished my confidence overall. None of those things are going to help anyone.

The cost of judgement and mum-shaming: isolation and anxiety

Mums shaming other mums: who would ever have thought that it would be a serious and mental-health-diminishing thing? Perhaps it's been going on for centuries. Perhaps Neanderthal women used to sit around the fire, bitching about how such-and-such's little Rocky was roaming about, throwing spears at passing woolly rhinoceroses. Or sneakily painting random cave walls with rude pictures. Or not even crawling yet. It's hard to know.

What I do know is that some women reach deep down into the most insecure and negative parts of themselves and pluck out mean things to say about the mums they know. And the mums they don't know. Really, *any* mum will do for these women!

You may have witnessed their behaviour or even been the target of it. Maybe you have even dabbled in a bit of it yourself.

Some 2019 research led by Kelly Odenweller, assistant teaching professor of communication studies at Iowa State University, found that women tend to group other mums into one of seven different stereotypes:

Ideal

Lazy

Overworked

Traditional

Non-traditional

Home- and family-oriented

Hardworking and balanced

I feel like I've been all of these at one time or another, but that is by the by.

The mums who fell into the 'lazy' or 'ideal' mum stereotypes were the least liked. Further, the research participants said that they would treat a lazy or ideal mum poorly, by excluding her, arguing with or even verbally attacking her. What. In. The. World?

Granted, this was a small study of 500 women, but you do see this sort of thing playing out on social media very, very often. My completely anecdotal observation is that the more 'high profile' the mum is, the more criticism is thrown in her direction.

Kelly told website *ScienceDaily* that negative interactions with other mums can have a significant effect on a mum's wellbeing, especially if she is already feeling pretty low. 'It's not unusual for moms to have low self-esteem or feel they're not living up to the standards of what it means to be a mom. If other moms treat them poorly, even when they're trying to do a good job, they may feel they can't turn to other people in their community for support.' This can cause isolation, anxiety and depression in said mum, affecting not only her but also her children and partner (if she has one). Even one snarky comment can spark this cascade of negative consequences.

Kelly says that – unfortunately – it's sometimes mums who appear to embody all sorts of 'good mum' behaviours that are snarking on other mums. Clearly those mum-shamers need to cease and desist this instant. Muttering something about 'toughening up' or 'being too thin-skinned' is not going to cut it.

Can't we just be kind to all the mums? Can't we give them credit for the hard job they're doing? After all, as Theodore Roosevelt said, 'The man who really counts in the world is the doer, not the mere critic – the man who actually does the work, even if roughly and imperfectly, not the man who only talks or writes about how it ought to be done.'

Dear Pip

'Someone judged me and I feel crap. What next?'

It's not always possible to simply ignore the judgement of others. And in my book, it's not healthy – much better to think about punching your critic in the nose. JUST KIDDING. It's better to surface the feelings you are having about the criticism and look them square in the eye.

Feelings have a way of being easier to process when we notice and address them. I highly recommend talking yourself through a process like this:

1. Document: 'CrunchyMama696969 said that I should stop posing for selfies and put a hat on my child and it cut me to the core. I feel so embarrassed.'

2. Clarify: 'Ugh. I'm a bit mortified. My face feels hot every time I think of it. I should have put a hat on Daisy, it's true. I hate being called out publicly. I feel worried that others are judging me, too. This makes me feel like everyone hates me and I'm a bad mum.'

3. Accept … and move on: 'I did make a mistake, but all humans make mistakes. I'm not a bad mum. People don't hate me. It's interesting that someone would decide to comment so publicly, rather than letting me know their thoughts privately. Would someone I really care about and am close to do that? No, they wouldn't. I can work on letting this pass. I am doing my best. This is not a big deal in the scheme of things. This time next week, it won't make me feel this way.'

The cost of comparison: isolation and anxiety

We hear a lot about the effects of social media on body image – and quite rightly so – but there's so much more to the comparison game than that. Not only can we choose to compare our bodies to those of other humans, we can compare our lifestyles, parenting and mental health, too. It's a very slippery slope and one that most of us do our level best to avoid heading down. But we don't always succeed.

So, what to do? How can you begin to shift this tricky relationship with social media and feel happier to be yourself?

Detoxifying your social media feed is a great place to start.

Research has found that mixing up what we're looking at on social media can help us to feel better about ourselves and our lives. The experts suggest loading your newsfeed with plenty of quotes focused on self-compassion, images of natural environments and, of course, plenty of cute animals. Bring on the cats!

Social media was deliberately built to mess with our minds, so it's no surprise that it's delivering on that goal. Sean Parker was Facebook's founding president and he freely admits that the platform was explicitly designed to exploit our vulnerabilities. In 2017, he told *The Guardian* that when Facebook was being developed, the focus was: 'How do we consume as much of your time and conscious attention as possible?'

The 'like button' that rules the algorithms of social media was one of those attention-grabbing features. It was designed to give users a little dopamine hit, training them to continue to interact with the platform and associate it with pleasure. That sounds pretty harmless, but Parker explained (apologetically, apparently) how it exploits a vulnerability in our psychology. 'It literally changes your relationship with society, with each other. It probably interferes with productivity in weird ways. God only knows what it's doing to our children's brains.'

The old 'won't someone think of the children?' shtick doesn't really cut the mustard with me, Mr Parker. Any product aimed at exploiting a human vulnerability is questionable. (And also, won't someone think of the mums? And the dads? And the grannies? Everybody counts.)

Facebook and Instagram (which is now owned by Facebook, as you probably know) both work on this very effective social-validation feedback loop foundation. It's so effective that, in 2017, the UK's Royal Society for Public Health described social media as being more addictive than cigarettes and alcohol.

Tired, isolated, time-pressured, lonely, 'trying to be good' mums are particularly vulnerable to these platforms' pitfalls. While they're the places mothers might document their lives and find inspiration, they're also the very same places that they might find themselves being judged, comparing themselves to the oft-touted 'highlights reel' of other parents' lives … and regularly falling short.

Social media is often bad for us. Its use has been correlated with sleep problems, negative body image, anxiety, depression and cyberbullying. We're also getting a daily mega-dose of 'social comparison' delivered straight to our phones and it's not doing us any good.

Back in the 1950s, social psychologist Leon Festinger began floating a theory about social comparison and how we build our sense of self by observing and comparing ourselves to others. He could not have known that we'd be served this comparison game on steroids 60-odd years later.

Leon noted that we like to make downward social comparisons with people who seem to be worse off or less skilled than us. This boosts our self-esteem, he observed. (Not very nice, but we all know it's a thing and plenty of people DO do this.) The flipside is that when we compare ourselves to those who we think might be better off or more skilled than we are, our self-esteem takes a hit.

If we're doing this several times a day, every day ... well, you can see how terribly this can impact us and why it can lead to anxiety, depression and all those other shitty things. Other social side effects include fear of missing out (FOMO), reduced attention span, acting out for 'likes', self-absorption and withdrawing from offline activities and interactions.

Researchers have noted that social media can be terribly inauthentic and very performative. Users often adopt a persona when they post, showing their ideal or most engaging selves – they've applied a generous helping of the old 'razzle-dazzle'. So those comparisons some of us are making? You may as well compare yourself to a fictional character of your choice. Hermione, anyone? Pippi Longstocking, perhaps?

While we *can* easily connect to others on the socials, it's important to remember that these platforms are – at their (black) heart – focused on curating image and reputation, and collecting and selling the data of the addicted humans who use them. Shudder.

'They are called Facebook, YouTube or MySpace and not WeBook, OurTube or OurSpace because they are all about the self-presentation of the individual (networked) self,' the University of Westminster's Professor Christian Fuchs wrote in his 2017 paper, 'Social Media: A Critical Introduction'. In other words, they're designed to be performative, rather than build meaningful relationships.

And then there are those 'status updates' that indicate what social media is really all about. Let's all build our social status! Um …

I'm telling you all this because, make no mistake, if you are feeling miserable, excluded and 'less than' when you spend time on social media, that is a VERY NORMAL response.

Social media is often NOT a wholesome place. It's built on some pretty shitty foundations and designed to manipulate you for profit. No wonder you are feeling a bit rubbish about it.

That's not to say it's all bad. Indeed, it is not. Very often it's a valuable connector between exhausted mums and their friends, peers, family members and like-minded folk. But it *is* to say that you MUST be careful with yourself when you use the socials. Try not to buy into the dopamine hit and the measuring thing and the general sneaky nonsense.

You're not the only one

Clearly you (possibly) and I (definitely) are not the only ones struggling with the good and the less good of social media.

I spoke to some of my friends about how they felt after being online and scrolling through the feeds of other parents. Here is what they said:

'I don't follow any other mums as I find it too difficult mental healthwise. I used to when my son was a baby and the pressure was too much for me. I have health problems and chronic pain, which means I'm tired most of the time and sometimes need to lie down. This makes me feel like a crap mum as I can't always do what I want to do with my son, we can't always be active and I have to limit the amount that I do so I can keep functioning. It's hard not to feel jealous of normal mums who have energy and strength!' – **Rabia**

'When I see beautiful images of bright clean homes I feel rotten. When I see posts about glorious days spent with the kids, especially during lockdown, whereas I have busied myself with chores or used my computer as escapism (even though I genuinely am teaching myself particular things on there), well, my heart hurts.' – **Linda**

'Their neat, colour-matched kids always baffled me. My own insisted on dressing themselves in mismatched colour combos from a very young age, then rolling around in the mud to accessorise. Perhaps if I'd only ever bought clothes in shades of brown, it might have been achievable?' – **Bron**

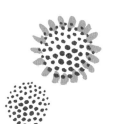

'I see so many Instagrammers with kids and tidy houses and wish I was one of those.' – **Rachel**

Long live the imperfect mum

A lot of us are feeling the way my friends are feeling. A 2020 UK survey into how women viewed 'mummy bloggers' found that:

23 per cent of those surveyed said that they find parenting influencers difficult to trust.

•

20 per cent of those surveyed thought parenting influencers painted an unrealistic view of mum life and made them feel pressured to be 'more perfect'.

•

10 per cent of respondents had unfollowed 'perfect mums'.

'These posts never show the days where you are covered in wee or sick,' one mum commented on parenting forum Mumsnet. 'Or the days when you are so tired that you yelled at your toddler for following you to the bathroom. Is it just me who thinks these so-called perfect parents are actually more damaging than helpful?'

'I follow a lot of Insta mums, too,' another mum posted. 'To be honest it started getting me down – they are all so perfect with perfect houses and lives, with every child-related gadget going because they are given it to endorse. I'm happy with my lot, don't get me wrong, but I find it depressing because I can't relate, either!'

See? Not. Just. You. Let's focus on non-perfect, closer-to-authentic, more human, healthy and sincere ways of being online.

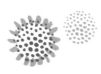

Getting real

There have been a slew of excellent campaigns aimed at providing a more realistic view of life on social media. They hope to bridge the gap between the humans we are and the humans we see as we scroll our newsfeeds, boosting our mental wellbeing in the process.

'Take a picture of yourself – or whatever is around you – showing the reality of your life using the #MyUnfilteredLife or #PowerofOkay hashtag,' mental health organisation *See Me Scotland* urged as part of one such brilliant campaign back in 2016.

The #ParentingUnfiltered hashtag on Instagram hopes to lead a similar push towards fewer artfully scattered Legos and more snotty noses … although I'm not really sure it delivers on the promise. (Why not post your own hashtagged snotty noses, filthy car seats and angry teenagers to tip things back into balance?)

In our fight against the monster that comparison can be, it would serve us well to think really carefully about how the internet makes us feel and what will truly serve us best.

Think about the way you engage with social media. Think about what makes social media use more fun and less fraught. And don't blame yourself for wrestling with this stuff. It's big stuff. It's an uphill battle that writer Alex Riley described in a 2018 *BBC Future* article like this: 'Learning how to manage my time on social media is like finding the right antidepressant.'

Social media self-assessment

Write down the pros and cons
of your social media habits.

Healthy social media use 101

Social media can provide a bunch of benefits if you are mindful of how you use it. Here are some ideas that might help to make your feed a more positive place to be.

Back away from the comparisons. Clearly they are unhealthy for all involved.

Unfollow accounts that make you feel terrible.

Use social media as a second-best way to manage your relationships (with 'in real life' ways of communicating being optimal).

Try using voice calls, video chats or good old snail mail to communicate with your pals.

Focus on connection on social media, not consumption.

If you find that you can't stop checking social media (to your detriment), try a time-limiting app, such as Forest, or disable notifications to give yourself a break.

Avoid online drama – not your circus, not your monkeys, not worth getting involved and having your phone pinging back tit-for-tat notifications.

Bring your thoughts back to your own values and goals, rather than what you see scroll past.

Remember that everyone you follow is sharing their 'social media persona', not their real life or true self. There's no point comparing yourself to something that's not really, truly real.

Compassion for others on social media (and IRL!)

One way to begin to rail against the negative effects of social media is to model the sort of behaviour you'd like to be on the receiving end of. Craft your own social media compassion policy when it comes to others and their parenting.

If you want to screen grab and marvel at someone else's ace parenting with your friends … go right ahead!

If you want to critique someone else's parenting on social media … don't.

If you want to screen grab and snark about someone else's parenting with your friends … just don't.

If you want to send someone a mean DM about their parenting (or anything else) … do not do it.

If you want to congratulate someone on their life or parenting … do this!

If you want to 'like' a mean comment that another social media user has left about someone else/their parenting … why bother?

If you want to send someone a kind DM about their parenting (or anything else) … go for it!

If you want to 'like' a positive comment that another social media user has left about someone else or their parenting … LIKE AWAY!

Forward these guidelines to your family and friends (and those people who lurk about your social media account liking pointed comments), or create your own.

As you become clearer about your own personal online code of conduct, you can also share ideas with your kids about their behaviour on social media. Chances are – if they are of late primary or high school years – they will have some bright ideas that you can add to your list.

Clearly we are writing the rule book as we go here, but the whole shemozzle is most certainly due for a major rethink.

Irina Raicu is the director of the Internet Ethics program at the Markkula Center for Applied Ethics at Santa Clara University in California and knows a lot about this stuff. In a 2016 piece published on the ABC website, Irina wrote that in this age of 'cancel culture' and rampant shaming we should be more measured in our interactions. Rather than reacting swiftly to others online, it's better to take our time, do some thinking and carefully consider our responses. 'We can try to respond less publicly, at least at first,' she wrote. 'Give people a chance to clarify, explain, recant or apologize – *privately*.' Irina also suggested that if we aren't directly involved, it's better to leave it to the person who's been wronged to respond, rather than jumping in and magnifying the response. And, of course, we could do with more forgiveness on the internet.

Just be kind and human with the other humans and look after yourself online.

CHAPTER 10

YOU ARE
NOT ALONE

When you need
some expert help

Professional support can change your life

While I'd love to tell you that self-care, mindfulness and affirmations can cure all mum ills, that is simply not the case. Many of us are going to need some extra help from a mental health professional at some point in our lives and I want to demystify that process for you.

At one point in my recent life, on the tail end of years of untreated depression and anxiety, I had a bit of a breakdown. The depression and anxiety I had learned to tolerate escalated and I was not able to function the way I wanted to. My big feelings were intruding on my life and my relationships with the people I loved the most. I was crying A LOT, or else feeling numb. It was scary and made me feel very out of control.

I tried lots of different DIY strategies to feel better, but nothing really worked. For some reason, I thought that seeking help would make things worse, and that all the things I was going through would rise to the surface and sort of suffocate me. So I soldiered on and on and on … until I couldn't.

Having lived through this hard time, I want to save you from enduring the same. You don't have to wait until you are at breaking point (like I was) before you seek professional support. I truly believe that everyone can benefit from therapy.

Only around one in three Australians with mental health difficulties reaches out for help and I suspect the story is similar in other Western countries. This could be for all kinds of reasons, including lack of access, financial pressures and – unfortunately – also because some people still feel embarrassed or ashamed to ask for the help they need.

Some countries (such as Australia) have a number of mental health sessions covered by a national healthcare system, making them more affordable. In some cities and towns, you can access low-cost mental health support via community centres, hospitals and universities.

Your country will have a psychological association or society that will help you locate professionals in your area. Your doctor should also have ideas on how you can access mental health support that suits your budget. There are also various online support services that can point you in the right direction (see page 258).

It might sound like a lot of work, but it's worth it, I promise.

When I was at my crisis point, I felt embarrassed to ask for help. I was also sure that talking about what was going on with me would unleash even more anxiety and sadness. Thankfully, I was wrong!

How do you know it's time to get help?

There are a whole range of feelings you may experience when anxiety, depression and other mental illnesses come into play.

Maybe you can relate to feeling some of these ways: sad, tired, angry, negative, panicked, confused, on edge, shaky, hopeless, super sensitive, worthless, scared, disoriented, confused, forgetful, distracted or even nauseous. Sometimes repetitive and intrusive thoughts come into play.

When you are feeling this way, your body is telling you that it – and you – are under pressure and you need to take extra good care of yourself. Perhaps a combination of these things is making your life really hard. Or perhaps it's just one or two. Whichever it is, that is enough reason to speak to your doctor and/or a mental health expert. They can help you to develop strategies to feel better and will treat you with the kindness and compassion you deserve.

If you need further convincing, here are some of the things the experts say are signs of needing mental health care. If any of these persist for two weeks or more, it's time to get professional support.

SOME SIGNS THAT IT'S TIME TO SEEK MENTAL HEALTH CARE

Feelings of numbness and emptiness

Avoiding people or places

An inability to manage big feelings

Feeling unable to work or cope with everyday life

Feeling increasingly isolated

Becoming more accident prone

Feeling on edge, consistently anxious or easily startled

Persistent feelings of physical stress

Increasing your intake of alcohol or drugs

Persistent disturbed sleep

How does it feel when you first reach out for help?

It feels different for everyone, I am sure, but for me it made me even more anxious and upset. I should say from the get-go that I am a fix-it-yourself kind of person. I thought I could sort out all my issues by myself. But I reached a breaking point where I could not deal with my life and it was really impacting my kids. Strangely, I didn't mind my mental ill health impacting myself, but when my kids were suffering the brunt of it, I could ignore it no longer. Pretty typical mum priorities, right? Ugh. Do as I say, not as I do – get help early and live a much nicer life!

My 'get help' moment happened when I could not stop crying for no particular reason as I drove down the freeway with my bewildered son. I have since found out that 'car crying' is a thing several of my friends are familiar with, too. It seems that it's just one of the many signs that we have been pushed to near-breaking point and a sure sign (among others) that it's time to tap into some expert care.

I booked a long appointment with my doctor and felt very nervous about how to go about summing up what I needed. After lying awake thinking about it for many hours over many nights, I did what almost every busy and overwhelmed mother would do: I wrote a list.

I wrote down all my problems – both physical and emotional – in case I got tongue-tied or started to cry during my visit. Then I took my list and I went to the doctor. Let me tell you what that was like, in case you have not yet had the experience of fronting up and talking about your wonky mental health with a doctor.

Generally, once you are sitting opposite the doctor, they will get you to complete some kind of quiz to help work out just how terrible you are feeling. This is not the fun sort of quiz you might be used to (like 'Which Spice Girl are you?'). It's the sort of quiz where you try to document your feelings on a scale of one to five.

I completed the quiz while I was sobbing, so just know that that is a completely okay option!

There was something sobering about seeing just how awful I was feeling written in my own hand on a piece of paper. That said, it's totally for the best and if you find yourself in this position, you're in the Wonky Feelings Quiz Club with me. Solidarity, sister!

My doctor did not mind at all that I was sobbing through our appointment and she had lots of ideas about how to begin sorting out all the things on the list. We talked (well, I sort of sobbed and stuttered) and I left with a physical and mental healthcare plan. Part of that plan was a referral to a psychologist as well as some information about antidepressants, and a follow-up appointment.

I felt quiet and strange in the car on the way home. A little numb, if I'm honest. But luckily this was the perfect state to be in when I rang the psychologist, which I did as soon as I got home. She'd had a cancellation and asked if I would like to come the next day. I said I would like that very much, even though I didn't quite believe myself.

I arrived way too early for my appointment, as was my nature at the time, and spent a lot of time in the car park near my new psychologist's consulting rooms. But once I eventually found myself sitting in that sparse, neat room, I did not look back.

After a few pleasantries, I dove in and began the first of many chats about the things that were making my life feel mostly terrible. In my mind, I'd thought I would fall apart if I told someone what was making me feel terrible. I thought I would unravel into a messy pile and my life would be much, much harder. Nothing could be further from the truth. I found so much relief in talking to a person who was interested (and indeed paid) to listen. Better still, this person was *trained* to listen and had spent years learning about how humans work ... and how to make them feel better. Speaking to a caring type about what I was going through helped me to breathe a little more deeply, sleep a little more soundly and feel a little lighter with each visit.

Of course, I was lucky to have found my person right away. When you go (you *will* go, won't you?) you might start off a little more slowly than I did, to be sure you have found the right person. If you don't like the first person you speak to, let your doctor know and they'll help you find someone else. Once you've found your perfect psychologist match, you can go all in.

It took quite a lot of appointments for me to feel like I had said all of the things I wanted to say out loud. This unburdening (and some antidepressants) helped to shift the way I was feeling about myself and the world around me. The crying stopped, the panic and anxiety that were constant companions became easier to manage and I began to feel more hopeful about the future.

In retrospect, I could have gone to the doctor and talked about the hard time I was having years before I did. So don't wait like I did. Go when the hard times begin to get too hard. Heck, go even before they get too hard. Accessing health care is always a brilliant idea.

If depression, anxiety and other mental ill health are making your days really tricky and your relationships hard to navigate, this sort of expert intervention might help you, too.

Dear
Pip

'How can a professional help me?'

I had no clue how it would feel to seek support for my mental health. I thought I did. I thought it was going to feel awful and exposing, but it felt like a huge relief. It felt like I could finally be myself after years of holding myself together with sticky tape and hope.

Here are some important things I want you to know about going to see a mental health professional.

You are partnering with your psychologist, counsellor or psychiatrist in the name of better health. You are a team!

Sessions are not designed to expose, judge or find fault in any way. Rather, your therapist will advocate for you, listen to you, help you make sense of your feelings and thoughts, and find ways to assist.

Despite what you see in the movies, there is usually not a couch for you to lie down on. This is sad for those of us who are exhausted. But seriously, it's not like that AT ALL.

If you feel uncomfortable with your therapist, talk to your doctor about finding someone you are able to trust and relate well to.

Therapy is amazingly helpful and you should not hesitate to ask your doctor for a referral. Tell them I sent you!

My psychologist, Christina, helped me develop strategies for looking after myself, shared ideas about self-compassion that made a lot of sense, and gave me permission to take my time when it came to getting better.

My friend Kerry Athanasiadis is also a psychologist. She describes her relationship with her clients beautifully: 'It is a great privilege to hold space for you and to hear your story.'

When I asked her, 'What would you tell a person who was a bit scared about the idea of reaching out for help from a psychologist?', she had heaps of ideas:

Feeling nervous is really normal. Who wouldn't feel nervous talking to a stranger about personal things? If you feel nervous, that is a completely rational way to feel.

The first session with a psychologist (or other mental health professional) is a 'getting to know you' situation. Your therapist will aim to get an understanding of your life and the people in it.

Near to the end of this first session, you and your therapist will likely set some goals outlining what you'd like to achieve from these appointments. You don't have to go into a lot of detail but rather give a summary. You can dive deeper next time.

Sessions can be conducted via video or phone (at least in Australia). This can be really helpful if you are feeling worried about navigating a first session (or any subsequent session) in person.

There are a
number of different ways
therapy can help and your person
will tailor your treatment to suit you.
You might just want to talk things through.
You might want your therapist to set you
helpful tasks to do between appointments.
You might want a mixture of approaches. You
might have your own ideas to share with your
therapist. All of these approaches are great.
Your sessions are designed to fit you and
your needs. If you don't know what your
needs are, your therapist can help
you work that out, too.

In future
sessions, you may feel
embarrassed to talk about
the things that are making life
difficult. It's important to understand
that your psychologist will never judge
and to remember that they have
heard many, many stories during
their professional career. Every
one of them is important and
deserves compassion,
never criticism.

THERAPY FAQS

How long does a session at the psychologist last for?

Between 50 and 55 minutes, generally. That might sound like ages, but the time usually flies by because there are LOTS of feelings and experiences to unpack.

How much will it cost?

It depends on where you live, but your country's psychologists' organisation or your doctor can advise you on this. Part of my sessions was covered by government health care, but I paid around $50 per session on top of that. I could not afford that, but I also could not afford not to go, so I tightened the budget in other areas and made it work.

How can I get the most out of my sessions?

Realise that mental and physical health care are equally important. If you would prioritise getting a broken ankle treated, you should do the same with your misfiring brain. These sessions are aimed at treating and easing your suffering. What could be more important than that?

Helpful tips for therapy newbies

I was a bit frightened of where life was taking me, so my sessions felt like a lifeline. Getting the right support made me feel strong enough to push on, took the edge off my suffering and slowly provided much-needed hope for the future.

Turn up to all your appointments. It can help to have some ideas on what you'd like to talk about, but even if you draw a blank, your therapist will know where to start.

•

Try to implement the ideas you talk about in your sessions. I wish I had taken notes during my chats with Christina, so perhaps that might help you to take the mental health strategies you discuss back out into the real world.

•

If you've read up to here, you will know that mental and physical health are intertwined. Be sure to care for your physical health as best you can as you undergo mental health therapy.

•

When strategies have worked, let your therapist know. Keep the feedback flowing so you can work together to make things better.

•

Know that mental health challenges can be treated and many people find treatment improves their lives immeasurably.

I found that having someone to talk to who was available, interested and clever was such a relief. You can't always rely on friends and family to have an available ear, and they can get a bit worn out when things are super tough. Calling in a professional can take some of the pressure off those relationships. It's a really brilliant thing to do for yourself (and your family) if you are in a position to do so.

THE FEELING AFTERWARDS

I asked my friends to describe the experience of therapy in one word.
Here is what they said:

exhaling

enlightening

empowering

loosening

unburdening

revelatory

bolstering

life-changing

grounding

motivating

clarifying

freeing

confronting

liberating

validating

Family violence: when your problems feel insurmountable

If you have found yourself in a position where you are feeling threatened or experiencing abuse, reaching out can feel impossible. Please know that there are professionals at the ready to support you. Also know that it can take some time to feel that you are able to seek this support.

Many, many women find themselves trapped in abusive relationships and it's through no fault of their own. One in four Australian women has experienced physical or sexual violence by a current or former intimate partner since the age of fifteen, and one in four Australian women has experienced emotional abuse by a current or former partner.

Sadly, the statistics are reflected in other countries. The UK's National Domestic Abuse Helpline tells us that, in the United Kingdom, one woman in four will experience domestic abuse over the course of her lifetime. In the United States, the National Domestic Violence Hotline says that intimate partner violence affects more than 12 million people each year.

The fact remains that there is no excuse for abuse. Women and children do not EVER deserve to be harmed.

There are a number of different types of abuse and all are incredibly harmful and damage women's lives. Some women are subjected to a number of types of abuse by the person they're in a relationship with.

Physical abuse: when someone hurts you, drives dangerously to scare you, throws things, restrains you or threatens to harm those you care about or animals/pets.

Sexual abuse: when someone involves you in non-consensual sexual activity, pressures you to have sex or pressures you into sexual activities that you are not comfortable with.

Emotional abuse: when someone threatens self-harm or suicide to manipulate you, threatens to prevent access to your children, criticises you, shames you, puts you down, constantly lies, tries to damage your reputation, is jealous or possessive of you, intimidates you, plays mind games, controls what you wear or coercively controls you.

Social abuse: when someone prevents you from seeing those closest to you, constantly checks up on you or interferes with your work and/or social life.

Financial abuse: when someone incurs debts in your name, refuses to work, refuses to contribute financially and/or controls your finances.

Tech abuse: when someone sends you abusive texts, forces access to your devices, tracks you with spyware or shares images of you without your consent.

Stalking: when a partner, ex-partner or someone else tracks you, follows you and/or forces unwanted contact with you.

**Being in an
abusive relationship
is incredibly isolating.
You may find yourself:**

· scared to confide in others
· blaming yourself
· feeling depressed and anxious
· feeling confused.

**You may have tried
lots of different strategies
to stop the abuse, such as:**

· trying to comply with your abuser
· avoiding your friends and family
· changing your own behaviour
· talking to your abuser about
the impact of their behaviour
· fighting back.

When abuse is happening at home, women may feel that any move they make could put their children or themselves in danger.

For women living in an abusive relationship, it's super important to maintain as many close relationships with family and friends as possible. Even if you are unable to talk to your nearest and dearest about what is happening at the moment, you may be able to tell someone in the near future. The people who love you will want to help you, if you give them the chance.

It's also vital that you find ways to care for yourself within the confines of your relationship. And that you know that when it feels possible, support is at the ready.

If you are in a relationship that makes you feel threatened, scared or controlled, I am so sorry that you are enduring that. It is such a terrible bind to be in, and balancing everyone's wellbeing in such a situation is very, very complex.

If you feel able to, you can talk to a counsellor via the domestic violence support services listed here, or Lifeline, Samaritans or similar in your country (see page 41). Your doctor can also help you to access safe support, if you are able to confide in them.

Just remember that you deserve a hopeful, joyful, meaningful and rewarding life.

Australia

National Sexual Assault,
Domestic Family Violence
Counselling Service

www.1800respect.org.au
or 1800 RESPECT
(1800 737 732)

Canada

Shelter Safe

www.sheltersafe.ca

New Zealand

Shine (Safer Homes in
New Zealand Everyday)

www.2shine.org.nz
or 0508 744 633

United States

National Domestic
Violence Hotline

www.thehotline.org
or 1-800-799-SAFE
(1-800-799-7233)

United Kingdom

National Domestic
Abuse Helpline

www.nationaldahelpline.org.uk
or 0808 2000 247

CHAPTER 11

DIAMOND DAYS AHEAD

*When you're wondering
if there's more to life*

What do you really, REALLY want?

Do you ever feel like you don't know how to be yourself? Or that your work and family's needs have taken up so much of your time that when you get a minute to yourself you become overwhelmed trying to work out how to spend it?

This, my friend, is a bit of a mum thing and in this chapter we're going to zero back in on the things that you love doing and start to focus on your own hopes and dreams. They might not be big things. One of mine, for instance, is to see a whale in real life, flip-flopping its giant tail in the ocean. Perhaps yours is to talk to an otter. Or to be able to name most of the constellations in a clear night sky. Or to run 20 kilometres without completely breaking yourself. Or to volunteer in an animal shelter where you can love all the pups and kittens freely.

I also have bigger dreams, of course. One is to write a bestselling feel-good novel about female friendships – the kind you'd see in the airport bookshop or see someone reading and giggling at on the bus. Perhaps you have big dreams, too. A career change? A sea change? A tree change? Some further study? Some changes in your family? You will likely have an inkling of your own big dream, but it's okay if you don't.

Sometimes we're so bogged down in the minutiae of day-to-day life that our curious, positive, imaginative selves get a little lost. I would like to encourage you to wake up said self and read on for some helpful ideas on getting back in touch with those important bits of you.

Get out your pen and notebook because there's lots of good stuff to scribble down.

Your best bits are your masterplan

Remember when we talked about your strengths back in Chapter 7? Let's talk about them some more and think about how you might apply them to the future things you're keen to do.

If you're keen to rethink your strengths and you'd like a little help, head to www.truity.com/test/personal-strengths-inventory to take a brilliant free quiz (or do an internet search for '24 personal strengths test').

These tests are based on the excellent work of prolific author and former president of the American Psychological Association, psychologist Martin Seligman and his colleague Christopher Peterson, former professor at the University of Michigan. These gents are both pivotal researchers in the field of positive psychology and they came up with a pretty definitive list of 24 signature strengths that humans may exhibit.

Turn over for my very brief cheat sheet on those core strengths, according to Seligman and Peterson. Perhaps you'll recognise a bunch of bits of yourself!

Strengths of **wisdom and knowledge**
facilitate learning and sharing of
knowledge and include things such as:

· creativity

· curiosity

· open-mindedness

· perspective

· a love of learning.

Strengths of **courage**
help us to accomplish goals, often
in the face of opposition.
They include skills such as:

· bravery

· persistence

· integrity

· vitality.

Strengths of **humanity**
include interpersonal, social skills such as:

· love

· kindness

· social intelligence.

Strengths of **justice**
underpin a rewarding life within the
community and include things such as:

- citizenship
- fairness
- leadership.

Strengths of **temperance**
involve behavioural regulation and protect us
against excess and include things such as:

- forgiveness
- humility and modesty
- prudence
- self-regulation.

Strengths of **transcendence**
are all about our connection to the universe and
meaning. They include things such as:

- appreciation of beauty and excellence
- gratitude
- hope
- humour
- spirituality.

I'm not embarrassed to tell you that when I did my strengths test, I scored highly for good judgement, love of learning, curiosity, integrity, persistence, kindness, gratitude and humour. *Takes a bow.*

Think about whether your work, home life and hobbies are making good use of these strengths. The more you flex those best bits, the happier you will feel, so incorporating a more formal strength-flexing practice into your life is a really simple way of boosting your wellbeing. Once you've honed in on the ace bits of yourself, ask:

· Can I use one of my strengths sometime today?

· How have my strengths helped me to do well at work?

· Can I use one of these strengths to help others?

· Can I pinpoint a time today when I used a strength? How did it feel? Can I do more of this?

· Which favourite activities align with my strengths?

· What are my strength successes telling me about other activities that I might want to pursue?

· How can my strengths help me to build stronger and more meaningful relationships?

· Which strengths am I keen to model to my kids?

· How can these strengths help me carve out a meaningful future?

It's all part of the authenticity puzzle helping you to get to know, accept and grow closer to the excellent person you are – and closer to those around you in the process.

Work those important core strength muscles regularly and you will not only feel brilliant, you will feel much more like yourself and much less ambivalent/conflicted when challenges pop up. It's worth getting to know yourself – and your strengths – better.

Get curious

I believe that lifelong learning is vital and that we should all be spending our days looking for interesting things and finding out stuff. Think about when you were a child and you wobbled along the shore turning over rocks to see what was under them. Or swishing your hand through the seaweed in rockpools, feeling around for salty treasures. This is, I believe, how life should be approached long after we have grown up.

This turning over and looking at and wondering about is what is going to lead us from one interest to the next. It's going to help us discover things about the world we inhabit and chase after the ideas, places, people and things we are most passionate about. Not only that, because we have our offspring wandering in our wake, we are modelling this sort of curiosity to them and reinforcing that all that 'looking for treasure' they seem to do so easily is time well spent.

Your curiosity might be something you carry with you as you go about each day, or you might take things to a whole new level and enrol in some study that will see you asking (and answering) even more curly-yet-interesting questions.

Curiosity has a bunch of benefits above and beyond learning more about things. According to the Greater Good Science Center at UC Berkeley, curiosity has been correlated with greater happiness, engagement and work performance. It's also linked to increased empathy and stronger relationships. And, those who are curious have been helping us to observe and adapt, ensuring our own survival since day dot.

If you vow to be curious each day, you will find out more about the world around you and dig deeper into your relationships, learning more about the people you encounter. All of this leads to a clearer understanding of yourself and your value. And what could be better than that?

Live your values and find meaning

Another part of this 'who am I?' exploration involves pursuing the experiences and activities that give your life meaning. This meaning could be found in your home life or in your work life, or in both.

A sense of meaning or purpose seems to pop up when we are living in line with our core values. Sometimes mums are so tired that they can't quite remember exactly what values are.

Values are the things in life that mean the most to a person. Your values might be focused on friendship, community, family, experiences, achievements, integrity, finances, home, health, activities ... they can be focused on a whole bunch of things.

The more our lives align with the values that are important to us, the more chance we have of feeling happy and healthy.

So how the heck do you settle on your own core values? Why not examine this handy-dandy list of values I've prepared for you. Put a tick next to the ones that are the most meaningful to you.

A 'THINGS THAT MEAN THE MOST TO ME' LIST

- Love
- Wealth
- Wisdom
- Family
- Community
- Morals
- Success
- Education
- Power
- Compassion
- Friends
- Adventure

- Courage
- Calm
- Freedom
- Fun
- Health
- Security
- Recognition
- Nature
- Popularity
- Responsibility
- Honesty
- Home

- Diligence
- Humour
- Trustworthiness
- Loyalty
- Self-control
- Frugality
- Independence
- Achievement
- Beauty
- Art
- Empathy
- Ambition

- Humility
- Self-awareness
- Wanderlust
- Environmentalism
- Spirituality
- Respect
- Romance
- Stability
- Fairness
- Acceptance
- Creativity
- Safety

Some of the values you choose might reveal a bit of a theme. For instance, if you chose 'trustworthiness' and 'loyalty' and 'honesty', you might group those under the core value of INTEGRITY.

If you chose 'creativity' and 'art' and 'beauty', perhaps those could be grouped as a core value of EXTREME CREATIVITY!

'Security', 'wealth' and 'frugality' might indicate a core value of FINANCIAL HEALTH.

The point is, these are your values and you get to make this stuff up. You might never have really thought deeply about who you are and the things that mean the most to you. Or maybe you did, but it was back in high school and things have changed just a bit since then. No matter, though, because the time is ripe to consider your good self in a fresh light. It's time for a values update.

Look for the patterns in the values you chose from the list on page 239 and see if you can find ways to categorise the like things to make the essence of you and your values clearer.

My core values would see me striving to be compassionate, trustworthy, pragmatically optimistic and serving others. I admit that we're hacking this values thing a tiny bit to make it work for us and I'm not the least bit sorry. 'Pragmatically optimistic' is absolutely a value!

'Best life' ingredients

We know (because research confirms it) that when we have meaning in our lives, we do better. Values are part of that meaning, but some other elements are also important, as Lisa A. Williams of the School of Psychology at the University of New South Wales wrote in a 2019 piece for *The Conversation*. In her article, 'Having a sense of meaning in life is good for you – so how do you get one?', she explained that purpose, significance and coherence help us to find our place in the world.

Let's dig a little deeper into those, so you can work those important things into your days.

Purpose

This means that we have goals and direction.
Your direction and goals will likely be influenced
by, you guessed it ... your values!

Significance

Humans need to feel that their lives have worth and value.
Living in line with your values can bolster this sense of
significance. See how important this values thing is?

Coherence

Coherence means that your life has some sort of
predictable routine. This is not always logistically
possible, but it is possible if we see our lives as
a set of values we're putting into practice.
Another big tick for values!

But there's even more value to values. A University College London longitudinal study of over 7000 UK folk (who all happened to be over 50) found that those who reported 'higher meaning in life' maintained healthier habits than those who did not. They stayed in touch with friends more, were part of social groups, volunteered in the community and had better sleep, diet and exercise habits. In other words, they stayed aligned with ... their values. They made time for the things that were most important to their lives (admittedly, they didn't have children to contend with, so you will have an extra degree of difficulty, but PUSH ON – I know you can!).

Don't delay in putting together that core values list – and thinking about how you can bring those values into play in your own life.

Dear Pip

'What about all the hurdles?'

Are you feeling a bit huffy because this whole 'living your values' and 'making the most of your strengths' and 'doing the things you most want' seems pretty impossible?

I get it, I truly do. There are often some tricky bits in between the things we want to do and where we are. Those bits might be lack of time, lack of money, lack of child care, lack of energy, lack of support, lack of health, lack of something else.

I totally understand. I have put off way too many things myself because it felt impossible to create the opportunities to do those things. My responsibilities and circumstances seemed a bit impenetrable, which is why you see me starting a degree now, much later in life than was necessary. Anxiety, depression, a light-on support crew and other tricky circumstances got between me and the things I wanted to do.

I started doing my 'most wanted' things when I hit 40. My kids were a bit older then and I just got fed up with putting my hopes and dreams last. You might be feeling a bit fed up, too. (Or maybe you are completely happy with the way life is humming along right now. That is totally okay, too!)

What I am telling you is that you should give yourself a serious talking to and find out whether you are putting off your 'things' because you are really, truly not ready for them (due to circumstance or other), or because you are feeling like you don't deserve to do them.

If it's the latter, in any way, shape or form, please give yourself the gift of doing the things you want to do. Life is so very short and you absolutely deserve all the happiness and interesting experiences you can cram in.

If you take time to follow your own interests and curiosities, your kids will adjust. In the long run – playing the long game – they want a happy mum. When they are grown-ups, they are not going to say 'you were always doing uni homework' or 'you went off on that hike and grandma tucked me in and I cried!' or 'you were always planting vegetables in the garden, dammit!'.

Instead they will say 'remember when we all had cereal for dinner and watched *Ghostbusters* three times in a row' and 'I hardly ever heard you fart!' and 'remember that one time a meatball rolled off the table and onto the floor?' and things like that.

BUT … if you are in a position where you really *cannot* move forward with the things you'd like to do just yet, take heart. Perhaps those things will be achievable down the track. For now, it could be a brilliant idea to start keeping a journal detailing these goals and working slowly towards them, when the time is right. It would also be brilliant if you could access some counselling if at all possible. Sometimes having a sounding board can help to open up things that seem pretty deadlocked. Many community health centres can help you find out more about accessing this type of support, as can your doctor.

The general idea is that you do what you can, when you can, to factor in some things that matter to you. Assembling a support crew – such as a counsellor or trusted friends or family – is key, too.

For many women, there are other significantly challenging factors that intervene between hopes and dreams, like traumatic relationships or mental or physical ill health. Mothers of children with a disability may need to take a slower road to achieve the things they most want. Women with low or no independent income may also have to think very strategically about their to-dos. I've been there myself, so don't feel that you will be 'stuck' forever.

If you're in a situation that is making your own needs pretty difficult to factor in, I'm so sorry to hear that. Just do what you can and remember that you are a precious person.

Some exercises to help you be yourself

I've pulled together a bunch of exercises that are designed to help you shift the focus back to YOU and help you find meaning where life might seem a little chaotic.

1. Write a short story of you

Write just ten lines that summarise the sort of person you are. Think carefully and don't be modest. You're the only person who is going to see this, so put it all down.

My short story would look a bit like this:

- I am sentimental, sensitive and strong.
- I am hardworking, motivated and resilient.
- I love my pets.
- I want my kids to be proud of me and know the value of perseverance and a good work ethic.
- I love learning, writing, cooking, making things and dreaming up bright ideas.
- The things I make and create have links to my childhood or they seek to create joy.
- I try to do my best.
- I prefer collaboration to competition.
- I want to work until I am 90 or more because I love creating and being useful.
- The older I get, the kinder to myself I am.

Yours will look different to mine, of course. If ever you're feeling lost, read your lines back to yourself. Remember who you are, what you're made of and what's at the heart of what you do.

The story of me (so far)

----

2. Craft your (loose) life rules

Getting a little bit more granular, think about how you *really* want to live your life and spend your days. Make a list of loose rules that focus on what's most important to you. This is a sort of next step from your core values and will detail how you're going to make those values a daily, practical practice.

For instance, my (loose) life rules look like this:

- Look after my health.
- Enjoy quiet times.
- Keep on learning.
- Prioritise creativity.
- Spend time with loved ones.
- Improve something every day.
- Try new things.
- Be curious.
- Do meaningful work.
- Celebrate happy moments.

And if you don't follow the rules? It's okay – that's why they are called LOOSE life rules.

You could encourage your kids to draw up their own list of rules – maybe you could all revisit your rules each year to see if they need updating.

3. Write your own mini-autobiography

The stories we tell about our lives can reveal more than the sum of their parts, so let's unpick them (carefully, if need be – it's fine to skip over any too-hard bits because this is about writing a story that feels helpful to you).

When you're a mother, your story instantly intertwines with that of your children, but it's really important to take a few steps back and consider what shaped you. This exercise can provide some excellent perspective, prompt some gentle self-back-pats and help you to better understand the way you live within your family.

SO DO IT! WRITE DOWN A COUPLE OF LINES (OR MORE) IN RESPONSE TO THE FOLLOWING PROMPTS:

- Talk about your childhood, what it was like, where you were raised, your family, pets, your home, your school/s.

- Write about some of the good things you did then, what made you happy, memories you might have, holidays, toys, friends.

- Write about growing up and studying or your first job.

- Write about when you first moved out of home.

- Have you travelled? Where to?

- What is life like now? Write about your friends, partner and family.

- What are the good things you are doing now?

- What are you most proud of?

- What are your hopes for the future?

You could even pull together an album of printed photos and other bits and bobs to help document your story.

EVEN MORE QUESTIONS THAT MAY HELP YOU FOCUS IN ON YOUR BIG AND SMALL HOPES AND DREAMS

When you were young, what did you want to be when you grew up?

What do you most love doing now?

How do you like to spend your spare time?

What makes you feel like a good human?

If money was no object, what would you be doing?

What activities make you feel the most energised and positive?

If you had a six-month sabbatical to do anything, what would you do?

What have you always been good at doing?

What do you wish you knew more about?

Which activities do you enjoy so much that you get lost in them?

What skills or strengths do others compliment you on?

By now, YOU should be coming into focus and you should be much clearer on what's most important to you – and how you can make time for the things that matter most. Hooray!

Where to next?

Let's finish by writing a bit of an action plan for everything that we've discovered and confirmed about you.

Make your plan concrete but flexible to factor yourself in, take good care of your ace self and aim for those diamond days (making your family's days more sparkly, too!). Because the fact remains that there is a trickle-down effect when women are doing well – kids also do better.

Thinking about all the exercises you've tackled here, what activities, tasks and experiences would you like to be making time for each day, week and month?

Daily tasks might be:

· read up on a favourite subject
· research further study
· plant and tend vegetables
· tuck $2 in a piggy bank
· spend fifteen minutes writing
· work on a crafty project
· spend fifteen minutes working on an online course.

Weekly tasks might be:

· go to an evening class
· run a longer distance than usual
· share my skills with someone
· volunteer in the community
· spend an hour in a cafe alone.

Monthly tasks might be:

· attend an appointment with a careers counsellor
· organise to see a therapist
· host a book club
· take a weekend away
· donate to a worthy non-profit organisation
· see a financial counsellor
· take a parenting class.

To make your own plan, write these headings across a page: Day, Week, Month. Underneath these, write your ideal to-dos, in line with all that you've discovered about your good self.

When mums
are feeling physically
and emotionally well and being
supported by those around them, they
are able to work on building lives that make
them feel nourished and stimulated. And they
feel hopeful. And they grow children who see
their mum doing things she loves. And they want
to do things they love, too. And they go out into
the world and do that, inspiring others to be
hopeful, happy and helpful. All because
you had the resilience and motivation
to make time for the things that
mattered to you.

Clearly
you are a
BLOODY BRILLIANT
mum!

RESOURCES

Playlist for mums who love their kids and also sometimes feel like running away from home

Can you encapsulate the highs and lows of parenting in a fun, feel-good playlist?

Yes, dear reader, I think you most certainly can!

'Nobody Told Me' John Lennon

'Three Little Birds' Bob Marley and the Wailers

'Everything I Wanted' Billie Eilish

'You Need to Calm Down' Taylor Swift

'Stronger' Kanye West

'Family Affair' Sly & the Family Stone

'Lovin' You' Minnie Riperton

'Comeback Kid' Sharon Van Etten

'Tiny Victories' Christina Perri

'Mad World' Lily Allen

'I'm Every Woman' Chaka Khan

'Run the World (Girls)' Beyoncé

'Nonstop' Drake

'Some Days Are Diamonds' John Denver

'Lovely Day' Bill Withers

'Let's Go to Bed' The Cure

'Army of Me' Björk

'Big Mistake' Natalie Imbruglia

'Guilty' Paloma Faith

'Heroes' David Bowie

'Sorry' Halsey

'Don't Stop Believin'' Journey

'Surrender' Cheap Trick

'Holiday' Madonna

'I Try' Macy Gray

'Lovely' Billie Eilish and Khalid

'Sorry' Justin Bieber

'All I Really Want to Do' Cher

'You Are the Sunshine of My Life' Stevie Wonder

'Feeling Good' Nina Simone

Reading list

I've made
you a handy list
of books that have
helped me, including books
that are mentioned in
Days Like These.

Perhaps you'd like to
add them to your
'to read' list!

A Mindfulness Guide for the Frazzled by Ruby Wax

The Artist's Way by Julia Cameron

Authentic Happiness by Martin Seligman

The Body Keeps the Score: Brain, Mind, and Body in the Healing of Trauma by Bessel Van der Kolk

The Book You Wish Your Parents Had Read (and Your Children Will Be Glad That You Did) by Philippa Perry

Craft for the Soul by Pip Lincolne

Daring Greatly by Brené Brown

Eat, Drink, Run: How I Got Fit Without Going Too Mad by Bryony Gordon

The Gifts of Imperfect Parenting by Brené Brown

The Happiness Project by Gretchen Rubin

Mama Rising: Discovering the New You Through Motherhood by Amy Taylor-Kabbaz

Maybe You Should Talk to Someone by Lori Gottlieb

The Motherhood edited by Jamila Rizvi

Motherhood & Creativity: The Divided Heart by Rachel Power

Of Woman Born: Motherhood as Experience and Institution by Adrienne Rich

The Pocket Pema Chödrön by Pema Chödrön

Resilient: How to Grow an Unshakable Core of Calm, Strength, and Happiness by Rick Hanson

Self-Compassion: The Proven Power of Being Kind to Yourself by Kristin Neff

The Self-Compassion Skills Workbook by Tim Desmond

The Well-Gardened Mind by Sue Stuart-Smith

Your Own Kind of Girl by Clare Bowditch

Support services

One of the things that really helped me to gain perspective and put a much more positive plan in place for my kids and myself was talking to mental health professionals. There are lots of different services that can connect you to the support you may need. Here are some excellent places to start.

Australia

Lifeline: 13 11 14
Beyond Blue: beyondblue.org.au
National Sexual Assault, Domestic Family Violence Counselling
Service: 1800 RESPECT (1800 737 732) or 1800respect.org.au

·

New Zealand

Lifeline: 0800 543 354
Shine (Safer Homes in New Zealand Everyday): 0508 744 633 or 2shine.org.nz

·

United Kingdom

Samaritans: 116 123
Heads Together: headstogether.org.uk
National Domestic Abuse Helpline: 0808 2000 247 or nationaldahelpline.org.uk

·

United States

Lifeline: 1 800 273 8255
National Domestic Violence Hotline: 1 800 799 SAFE (7233) or thehotline.org

·

Canada

SAM: 1 866 277 3553 (outside Montreal) or 514 723 4000 (Montreal)
Shelter Safe: sheltersafe.ca

·

International

Better Help: betterhelp.com

Thanks to ...

My excellent grown-up children Rin, Max and Ari ... always inspiring!

Bean, Peach, Olive and Chippy ... always fluffy!

The wonderful Jane Morrow, who listens and teaches me things.

Kristy Allen and Lou Playfair for their vision and their hard work on this book.

Champion word wranglers Julie Mazur Tribe and Justine Harding.

My favourite designer in the world, Michelle Mackintosh.

Kerry Athanasiadis, Associate Professor Christina Bryant and
Dr Jeannie Knapp for helping me understand more about mental
and physical wellbeing.

Steve Wide for the musical moral support.

My mum, and her mum, too.

My buddies and readers for constantly and helpfully egging me on.

Index

A

abusive relationships 225–229
accommodation (parenting style)
  80–81, 149
ambivalence about motherhood 70
anger as normal part of parenting 82–83
anxiety 27–29
aromatherapy 121

B

becoming a mother. *See* matrescence
bonding 69–70, 72
book list for mothers 257
breathing, deep, as self-care
  strategy 142
Byrne, Laura 75

C

calmness, benefits of maintaining
  94–95, 96
children, relationships with
  awareness of children's feelings in 62
  honest communication in 48–51
  positive parenting qualities to bring
    to 52–54
COVID-19 pandemic 176
creative activities as self-care
  strategy 124–125
criticism and judgement of mothers
  192–198. *See also* social media
curiosity, cultivating 237

D

dancing as self-care strategy 119
diary, keeping a 156–157

diet 112–113
domestic violence 225–229
domestic work. *See* household
  management and work

E

eating well 112–113
exercise as self-care strategy 120

F

family violence 225–229
feelings
  finding words to describe 61
  strategies for dealing with 62, 63,
    144–145, 198
forgiveness
  forgiving your child 143
  forgiving yourself 139–142
friendships with other mothers
  ideas for initiating 34
  importance of 22–25

G

gardening as self-care strategy 116
gender inequality 171–177
'good enough' parenting 78–79, 81, 148
guilt, feelings of 66–67
  finding perspective on 86–87
  guilt versus shame 137
  strategies for dealing with 83, 87
  typical experiences 133–134

H

Harry, Duke of Sussex 76
Hawkins, Jennifer 75
health issues, links between physical
  and mental 26–27, 29, 179

help and support. *See* support and help, providing to others; support and help, seeking from others

hormones. *See* stress hormones

household management and work
  being the default manager and worker 170–171
  fatigue resulting from 178
  gender inequality and 171–177
  sharing the load of 182, 184–185
  tasks involved in 178, 183

images of parenthood, idealised. *See* 'perfect' parenting, myth of

immune system, effects of stress on 20

inner critic. *See* self-talk, negative

isolation. *See* loneliness and isolation

Johnson, Matt (Matty J) 75

journal, keeping a 156–157

judgement and criticism of mothers 75–76, 192–198. *See also* social media

kindness to others as self-care strategy 122–123

loneliness and isolation 17–19
  friendships with other mothers, importance of in preventing 22–24
  as gateway to other problems 19–21
  health effects of 20–21, 114

love, demonstrating 99

love, unconditional 72

matrescence 68–70, 71, 82–83, 100–101

meaning and purpose, finding 240–241. *See also* personal growth; self-knowledge

meditation 142

Meghan, Duchess of Sussex 76

mental health issues. *See also* loneliness and isolation
  anxiety 27–29
  managing, as prelude to living a full life 35

mindfulness 97–98

'mistakes' in parenting 132
  guilt and shame arising from 135, 137–142
  what making mistakes feels like 133
  working through and learning from 134–136, 146–147

music playlist for mothers 255

nature, spending time in 115

needs, identifying your physical and emotional 30–33

newborns and toddlers, society's focus on 18

obstacles and setbacks, dealing with 242–243

over-parenting 148–149

overwhelmed, feelings of being. *See* stress

oxytocin 69–70

pandemic, COVID-19 176

panic attacks 27–28

parenting skills and qualities
  adults' memories of parents' skills 90–91
  celebrating your wins 150–151
  day-to-day tasks 151
  keeping calm 94–95

mindfulness 97–98

modelling positivity and
    gratitude 99

positive parenting qualities 52–54

showing love 99

what children need from parents
    88–89, 92

parenting styles. *See also* 'perfect'
parenting, myth of

    accommodation 80–81, 149

    'good enough' parenting 78–79,
        81, 148

    over-parenting 148–149

'perfect' parenting, myth of 74–75,
78–79

    social media images 77, 199, 203,
        204, 205

personal growth. *See also* matrescence;
self-knowledge

    goal setting 126–127

    growth through being a mother
        100–101

    needs, identifying your physical and
        emotional 30–33

perspective, finding and maintaining
86–87

    cherishing every moment
        102–105

    giving yourself credit 154–156

    motherhood as a marathon 10

    'what went well' exercise 158

pikelets, recipe for 93

Pink (singer) 75

playlist, musical, for mothers 255

positive parenting qualities 52–54.
See also parenting skills and qualities

purpose and meaning, finding 240–241.
See also personal growth; self-knowledge

S

self-care strategies 108, 128–129.
See also self-compassion;
self-supporting

    child-free time 108–110

    creative activities 124–125, 128–129

    dancing 119

    eating well 112–113

    exercising 120

    gardening 116

    maintaining social connections 114

    meditation and deep breathing 142

    practising kindness to others 122–123

    sensory therapy 121

    setting personal goals 126–127

    singing 117–119

    sleeping 111–112

    spending time in nature 115

self-compassion 162–167. *See also*
self-talk, negative

self-esteem 159–161, 197. *See also*
self-talk, negative

self-knowledge. *See also* personal growth

    finding meaning and purpose
        240–241

    identifying physical and emotional
        needs 30–33

    identifying strengths 233–236

    identifying values 238–241

    tools for developing 244–250

self-supporting. *See also* self-care
strategies

    definition 11–13

    strategies 14–15

self-talk, negative 60

    inner critic 159–161

    self-compassion 162–167

    strategies for dealing with 61–62,
        139–142

sensory therapy 121
shame, feelings of 132–133, 135,
137–142. *See also* guilt, feelings of;
judgement and criticism of mothers
singing as self-care strategy 117–119
single parents 186
skills for parenting. *See* parenting skills
and qualities
sleep 111–112
social connections. *See also* loneliness
and isolation
friendships with other mothers
22–25, 34
importance of 114
social media
campaign for authenticity in 205
comparing yourself to others on
199–205
compassionate use of 208, 209
healthy use of 207, 208
idealised images of parenting in 74,
77, 200–203
importance of to mothers 23–24
parent shaming on 75–76
solo parenting 186
strengths, identifying 233–236
stress
causes of 45, 144–145, 176, 177, 178
communicating with your kids about
48–51
health effects of 179
strategies for dealing with 46–47,
56–59, 144–145, 146–147, 180–181
stress hormones 20, 27, 28–29
what stress feels like 44, 55
support and help, providing to others
how to offer 36–39
kindness as self-care strategy 122–123
via social media 208–209

support and help, seeking from others.
See also therapy and other professional
support
contact details for support services
41, 258
how to ask for support, ideas on 34–35
importance of support 16–19, 35, 63,
187, 188–189
support from other mothers 22–25, 34

Teigen, Chrissy 75
therapy and other professional support
212–213
contact details for support services
41, 258
how a typical appointment might feel
216–218
tips for therapy newbies 223
typical cost 222
what to expect from 219–222, 224
when to seek help 214–215
'three good things' exercise 158
toddlers and newborns, society's focus
on 18
transition to motherhood.
See matrescence

unconditional love 72

values, identifying personal 238–241,
244–250
vulnerability, emotional 72–73

'what went well' exercise 158
wins in parenting, celebrating 150–151
women and gender inequality
171–177

Published in 2021 by Murdoch Books,
an imprint of Allen & Unwin

Murdoch Books Australia
83 Alexander Street
Crows Nest NSW 2065
Phone: +61 (0)2 8425 0100
murdochbooks.com.au
info@murdochbooks.com.au

Murdoch Books UK
Ormond House
26–27 Boswell Street
London WC1N 3JZ
Phone: +44 (0) 20 8785 5995
murdochbooks.co.uk
info@murdochbooks.co.uk

For corporate orders and
custom publishing, contact our
business development team at
salesenquiries@murdochbooks.com.au

Publisher: Jane Morrow
Editorial Manager: Julie Mazur Tribe
Design Manager: Kristy Allen
Designer: Michelle Mackintosh
Editor: Justine Harding
Production Director: Lou Playfair

Text © 2021 Pip Lincolne
The moral right of the author
has been asserted.
Design © 2021 Murdoch Books

ISBN 978 1 92235 139 5 Australia
ISBN 978 1 91166 822 0 UK

A catalogue record for this
book is available from the
National Library of Australia

A catalogue record for this book is
available from the British Library

Colour reproduction by Splitting Image
Colour Studio Pty Ltd, Clayton, Victoria

Printed by C & C Offset Printing Co. Ltd.,
China

10 9 8 7 6 5 4 3 2 1

MIX
Paper from
responsible sources
FSC® C008047